107 Awesome Elementary Teaching Ideas You Can Implement Tomorrow

107 Awesome Elementary Teaching Ideas You Can Implement Tomorrow contains a wide variety of effective, user-friendly strategies, tips, and activities for your elementary school classroom. Rich with anecdotes and examples, this resource features useful suggestions for creating a positive, cooperative classroom culture, improving academic instruction, and building student capacity. Specific topics include classroom management, social-emotional learning, language arts and math ideas, motivation and inspiration, family involvement, movement and mindfulness, and much more. You will also find printable pages, photographs, diagrams, and other helpful visual aids.

Bonus: The book's classroom-ready templates are also provided on our website as free eResources for ease of use.

Steve Reifman is a National Board Certified elementary school teacher, author, and speaker in Santa Monica, CA. Steve has written numerous resource books for educators and parents. He is also the creator of the award-winning Chase Manning Mystery Series for children 8–12 years of age. For teaching tips, articles, and other valuable resources and strategies on teaching the whole child, visit and subscribe at www.stevereifman.com. Follow Steve on Twitter (@stevereifman), "Like" his "Teaching the Whole Child" Facebook page, subscribe to his "Teaching Kids" YouTube channel, check out his two professional development courses for educators on Udemy.com, and visit his TeachersPayTeachers page.

T0384862

Also Available from Routledge Eye On Education
(www.routledge.com/k-12)

Activities, Games, and Assessment Strategies for the World Language Classroom, 2nd Edition
Amy Buttner Zimmer

Rigor in the K–5 ELA and Social Studies Classroom
Barbara R. Blackburn and Melissa Miles

Rigor in the K–5 Math and Science Classroom:
A Teacher Toolkit
Barbara R. Blackburn and Abbigail Armstrong

Creating a Language-Rich Math Class:
Strategies and Activities for Building Conceptual Understanding
Sandra L. Atkins

Math Running Records in Action:
A Framework for Assessing Basic Fact Fluency in Grades K–5
Nicki Newton

Everyday SEL in Elementary School:
Integrating Social-Emotional Learning and Mindfulness into the Classroom
Carla Tantillo Philibert

Close Reading in Elementary School:
Bringing Readers and Texts Together
Diana Sisson and Betsy Sisson

Family Math Night K–5:
Common Core State Standards in Action
Jennifer Taylor-Cox

Family Reading Night, 2nd edition
Darcy J. Hutchins, Joyce L. Epstein, and Marsha D. Greenfeld

107 Awesome Elementary Teaching Ideas You Can Implement Tomorrow

Steve Reifman

Routledge
Taylor & Francis Group

NEW YORK AND LONDON

First published 2020
by Routledge
52 Vanderbilt Avenue, New York, NY 10017

and by Routledge
2 Park Square, Milton Park, Abingdon, Oxon, OX14 4RN

Routledge is an imprint of the Taylor & Francis Group, an informa business

Library of Congress Cataloging-in-Publication Data
Names: Reifman, Steve, author.
Title: 107 awesome elementary teaching ideas you can implement tomorrow/Steve Reifman.
Description: New York, NY: Routledge, 2020. | Series: Routledge eye on education | Includes bibliographical references. | Identifiers: LCCN 2019048721 (print) | LCCN 2019048722 (ebook) | ISBN 9780367431709 (hardback) | ISBN 9780367431693 (paperback) | ISBN 9781003001676 (ebook)
Subjects: LCSH: Education, Elementary–Activity programs.
Classification: LCC LB1592 .R45 2020 (print) | LCC LB1592 (ebook) | DDC 371.4–dc23
LC record available at https://lccn.loc.gov/2019048721
LC ebook record available at https://lccn.loc.gov/2019048722

ISBN: 978-0-367-43170-9 (hbk)
ISBN: 978-0-367-43169-3 (pbk)
ISBN: 978-1-003-00167-6 (ebk)

Typeset in Berling and Futura
by Deanta Global Publishing Services, Chennai, India

Visit the eResources: www.routledge.com/9780367431693

To Mom, Dad, Lynn, Alan, Jeff, Sylvia, Ari, Jordy, and all the family, friends, teachers, and students whose support, expertise, and encouragement made this book possible

Contents

Part 2: Improve Academic Instruction 55

eResources

The templates can also be downloaded and printed for ease of use. Look for the eResources icon throughout the book. You can access these downloads by visiting the book product page on our website: www.routledge.com/9780367431693. Then click on the tab that says "eResources," and select the files. They will begin downloading to your computer.

Sample Quotes and Talking Points
Sample Biography from 2-Minute Biographies for Kids
Way to Go! Template
While You Were Absent
Three-Dimensional Character Bone Structure
Four-Color Editing Checklist
Problem Solving Organizer
Problem Solving Menu #1
Human Health Hunt
Place Value Unit Cover Sheet
Personal Narrative Reflection Sheet
How Do I Give Myself the Best Chance to Produce Quality Work?
General Scoring Rubric
Habits of Character Rubric

Meet the Author

Steve Reifman is a National Board Certified elementary school teacher, author, and speaker in Santa Monica, CA. During his 26-year career he has written several resource books for educators and parents, including *Rock It!*, *Changing Kids' Lives One Quote at a Time*, and *Eight Essentials for Empowered Teaching and Learning, K–8*. In addition, Steve has created a series of shorter, e-book resources for educators, including *10 Steps to Empowering Classroom Management*, *The First 10 Minutes: A Classroom Morning Routine that Reaches and Teaches the Whole Child*, *2-Minute Biographies for Kids: Inspirational Success Stories About 19 Famous People and the Importance of Education*, and *15 1/2 Ways to Personalize Learning*. He is also the creator of the award-winning *Chase Manning Mystery Series* for children 8–12 years of age. For teaching tips, articles, and other valuable resources and strategies on teaching the whole child, visit and subscribe at www. stevereifman.com. Follow Steve on Twitter (@stevereifman), "Like" his "Teaching the Whole Child" Facebook page, subscribe to his "Teaching Kids" YouTube channel, check out his two professional development courses for educators on Udemy.com, email him at sreifman@verizon.net, and visit his TeachersPayTeachers page.

Books by Steve Reifman

The Chase Manning Mystery Series
Chase Against Time (Chase Manning Mystery #1)
Chase for Home (Chase Manning Mystery #2)
Chase Under Pressure (Chase Manning Mystery #3)
Chase to the Finish (Chase Manning Mystery #4)
Chase on the Edge (Chase Manning Mystery #5)

Resource Books for Teachers and Parents
Changing Kids' Lives One Quote at a Time
2-Minute Biographies for Kids
22 Habits that Empower Students
10 Steps to Empowering Classroom Management
15 1/2 Ways to Personalize Learning
Rock It!: Transform Classroom Learning with Movement, Songs, and Stories
Eight Essentials for Empowered Teaching and Learning, K–8
The First 10 Minutes: A Classroom Morning Routine that Reaches and Teaches the Whole Child
The First Month of School: Start Your School Year with 4 Priorities in Mind
Build a Partnership with Parents
Math Problem Solving Menus
The Ultimate Mystery Writing Guide for Kids

Preface

During my 26 years as an elementary educator, I have worked to develop a "whole child" teaching approach that empowers students and emphasizes academic excellence, lasting Habits of Mind and Habits of Character, valuable work habits and social skills, and health and wellness. This book is a user-friendly compilation of what I believe to be the most effective, accessible ideas and strategies that I have shared in my print books, ebooks, YouTube videos, blog posts, and articles, plus many other ideas that are appearing for the first time. My goal is to make this resource as useful as possible for you.

Note: Some of the ideas I describe work best when we introduce them at the beginning of each new school year. If you happen to be reading this book in the middle or at the end of the year, it's no problem. The ideas will be effective whenever you incorporate them into your teaching practice.

Acknowledgments

Permission is gratefully acknowledged for use of ideas that were inspirational to the book:

Thank you to educator Andy Hair for allowing me to share some of his ideas that inspired Section 1, Idea 5) Silly reminders for things that need to go home.

Thank you to educator Jeff Haebig (www.pinterest.com/wellnessquest) for allowing me to share some of his ideas that inspired Section 5, Idea 34) Macarena Thursday; Section 13, Idea 72) "The Book Parts Song"; Section 16, Idea 95) Human Health Hunt; and Section 18, For Idea 107) Novelty.

Thank you to educator Chip Candy for allowing me to share some of his ideas that inspired Section 5, Idea 37) Reading Workshop Warmup.

Thank you to educator Debra Em Wilson for allowing me to share some of her ideas that inspired Section 5, Idea 36) Writing Workshop Warmup.

Thank you to Jean Moize (www.actionbasedlearning.com) who inspired Section 8, Idea 54) Active DLR (daily language review).

Thank you to Paul and Gail Dennison (www.HeartsatPlay.com) who inspired Section 5, Idea 35) Four-part movement warmup. The Cross Crawl and Hook-ups are part of Educational Kinesiology and the Brain Gym® Program by Dennison and Dennison, and are used here by permission. Brain Gym® is a registered trademark of Breakthroughs International/Educational Kinesiology Foundation (https://breakth roughsinternational.org/programs/the-brain-gym-program/).

Thank you to Elly Goldman and Denise Schiavone inspired Section 8, Idea 48) The Synonym–Antonym Sidestep.

Every effort was made to find the creators of the ideas and activities cited in this book. We apologize for any oversights.

PART 1

Create a Positive, Productive, and Cooperative Classroom Culture

Classroom Management Ideas

1) LEAD BY EXAMPLE

During my graduate training at UCLA, an instructor once remarked to our class that no matter what subject any of us went on to teach, we would all impact our students most powerfully with the examples that we set. He cautioned us not to lose sight of the fact that though we may teach science or English, more than anything else, we are teaching ourselves; we are teaching who and what we are. Years later, when students look back on the time spent in our rooms, they might not remember all the content. They will remember us.

As classroom teachers, we need to pay careful attention to the example we set for our students. This doesn't mean that we have to be perfect or that we should hold ourselves to some unrealistic standard. It does, however, mean that we make every effort to model for our students the qualities and behaviors that we promote. When leaders walk their walk, they accomplish a great deal more than they do with words alone.

Leading by example is by far the most powerful way to help children develop important academic and behavioral dispositions that I refer to as Habits of Mind and Habits of Character. Encouraging reflective thinking and incorporating self-evaluation and goal setting into our practice play an important role in our effort to help children internalize these ways of thinking and acting, but nothing matches the power of modeling.

Consider the habit of **honesty** for a moment. In the beginning of every school year, one of my main objectives is to create an environment of trust in my classroom, and that can only happen when everyone acts in an honest manner. What is the most effective way for me to promote honesty? Is it to establish a rule that everybody must be honest? No. It is to *be* honest. I must make and keep promises to my students so their trust in me grows. I show them how to be honest by modeling honesty every chance I get. Talking at my students will not achieve the same results. Leaders understand the power of a strong example.

Constantly look for ways to model Habits of Mind and Habits of Character for your students. Let your actions do the talking. For instance, to show how much you value **thoughtfulness**, provide students with "wait time" before having them answer a question. Pause for a few seconds before you answer their questions. Use a positive tone of voice, say *please* and *thank you* every chance you get, and look out for the well-being of others to encourage **kindness**. Demonstrate the high priority you place on **respect** by making eye contact with your students and listening closely when they speak to you. Share stories from your life about helping others to highlight the importance of **service**. Kids remember examples.

2) APPOINTMENT CLOCKS

An Appointment Clock is a classroom management tool that teachers can use in situations where students will be working in pairs. Appointment Clocks save valuable class time, empower kids to make meaningful choices, ensure that students have the opportunity to work with a variety of classmates, and facilitate smooth transitions.

Here's how Appointment Clocks work. Imagine that you are planning a classroom activity in which you would like your students to work in pairs. When you have finished explaining the directions and are ready for the kids to begin the activity, you ask everyone to find one partner and get started. Though this request may seem simple enough to follow, many students will struggle. Some may not feel comfortable approaching a classmate, others may not be able to decide how to choose one friend over another, and still others may choose the same friend every time you attempt cooperative learning. The potential exists for wasted time, hurt feelings, and a loss of focus from the activity itself.

All these potential problems can be avoided through the use of Appointment Clocks. This tool is simply a sheet of paper with a traditional clock printed on it. Though there are twelve hours on a clock, I have my students use only six of the hours at the beginning of the year (from 1:00 to 6:00).

Before asking my kids to fill the clocks out, I explain that everyone should use these sheets to record the names of six different people they would like to have as partners. I emphasize the importance of choosing people with whom they will get along and be able to focus. I have found that having six different partners on the clock works well for middle grade students because it ensures variety while still providing the opportunity to work with close friends frequently.

It usually takes about 15–20 minutes for the students to walk around and find their six partners. When almost all students have completed this task, I call them back together to check for accuracy. When I say "1:00", all the kids stand shoulder-to-shoulder with their 1:00 partners. If some students accidentally wrote a name in the wrong space or if some students do not yet have a 1:00 partner, we can make any corrections at this time. I proceed through all six hours of the clock until everything is correctly recorded. If necessary, some students may work with the same classmate for more than one hour on the clock, and if your class has an odd number of students (which is very different, by the way, than a number of odd students), each hour of the clock will contain a trio.

With our clocks complete, organizing cooperative learning is much easier. I attach a 1–6 spinner to the top of the white board. For our first pair activity I point the spinner to the "1" and have the kids work with their 1:00 partners. Next time around, I move the spinner to the "2" and ask everyone to work with their 2:00 partners. The spinner enables me to keep track of where we are in the sequence so that students work with all their partners the same number of times. It also keeps me from having to remember where we are in the sequence. Students will quickly memorize their six partners. Until they do, I have them tape a small list of their "Clock Partners" to the top corner of their desks for easy reference.

Now, for example, whenever I need students to work in pairs, I simply say, "You will work on this activity with your 4:00 partner." Our transition into the activity is a smooth one, and students are happy because they have the chance to work with someone that they, themselves, have chosen. I have found that there's a certain psychological comfort in this fact. Students are more invested in the activity because they were the ones who chose their six partners. Later in the year, I often have my students complete the rest of their Appointment Clocks so they have the opportunity to work with a wider variety of classmates. With these six new spaces on the clock, I'll allow them to repeat one or two of their original six partners.

3) 3-CLAP SIGNAL

One classroom management tool that all teachers need is a clear, simple, and reliable silent signal that we can use whenever we need our students' attention. Over the years I have found that the most effective option is what I call the "3-clap" signal. When I need everyone's attention, I clap three times. They respond by clapping three times at the same pace I used. After the kids clap, I say, "Empty hands on forehead, eyes on me, in 5, 4, 3, 2, 1, 0."

I speak calmly and slowly because many children feel stress when they hear a teacher's silent signal, and I want them to be relaxed. Some kids have trouble following silent signals because they want to keep working, and that's admirable. By counting down slowly, my goal is to provide everyone sufficient time to find a stopping point in whatever activity they're doing and give me their full attention. The "empty hands" part of the signal is important because it guarantees that they are no longer writing anything when they look at me.

Here are a few tips to keep in mind for any signal you decide to use. First, wait until you have everyone's full attention before beginning your instructions. Practice and emphasize this during the first few weeks of every school year so the kids know you are serious. After the first month of the year, if the kids continue working when you give the signal or talk when you're talking, hold them accountable by practicing this routine at the beginning of recess or lunch for a couple of minutes.

Next, try not to use your signal too frequently. Once children are in a groove and focusing well on an activity, we want to honor that. If we call for their attention every couple of minutes, we run the risk of interrupting their flow.

Finally, once you have given the signal and are about to provide directions, begin by saying, "When I say go." That way, the kids know to hear you out. Without these initial words, students will likely start carrying out your directions without hearing them in their entirety. As a result, the kids are unlikely to complete the directions successfully. Once you're done with the directions, then say "go." This is another skill that requires frequent practice at the beginning of each year. The hands stay on the forehead and the eyes stay on us until we say "go."

4) TABLE CARDS

On the days my students use their Writing Workshop notebooks, they begin by following our class routine of putting that day's topic at the top of the page in a box next to the date. Before I learned about Table Cards from a colleague a few years ago, I would give the kids a couple of minutes to carry out this task and then circulate throughout the room to ensure that everyone had headed their paper correctly. Using Table Cards saves me from this time-consuming endeavor while allowing the kids to take greater responsibility for their learning and build teamwork.

Here's how it works. You will need one index card per student, with every table receiving a different color. Imagine your class contains seven tables of four. You would need four red cards for Table 1, four blue cards for Table 2, four yellow cards for Table 3, etc. Each set of cards would be numbered 1–4, and the kids would always get the same color and same number. At the beginning of the period, I would ask all the 1s, for example, to serve as card monitors that day. (I keep a spinner on the board and rotate through the numbers so that the children each receive the same number of turns.)

The 1s would then take their set of cards and distribute them to their tablemates. Once every person at their table has finished heading their paper, the monitor checks for accuracy, collects the cards, and returns them to me. After I have received all seven sets, I know that the whole class has completed the routine. Of course, I need to teach this process at the start of the year and have everyone practice it for a few weeks before it becomes second nature. The use of Table Cards is not limited to Writing Workshop; we can employ this strategy any time we need to hold children accountable for completing written protocols.

5) SILLY REMINDERS FOR THINGS THAT NEED TO GO HOME

In my classroom we use the popular Words Their Way approach to improve our spelling skills. One night a week the kids take home their word strips in a Ziploc sandwich bag for a homework activity. Everyone is in the habit of taking home their independent reading books and reading notebooks every night, and these items are rarely forgotten. Taking home the bag of words, however, is not part of our nightly routine, and as a result, children sometimes leave their bags at school.

To remedy this problem, I started creating quick, silly reminders that have proven effective due to their novelty. The first is what I call the "Bag of Words Song." As the kids are packing up their belongings at the end of the day, we chant, in unison, "Bag of words, bag of words, bag of words." Some kids add rhythm and/or movement to this chant, and once we repeat it (way too) many times, everyone is smiling, laughing, and, most important, remembering to put their bag in their backpacks.

Recently, I added a second silly strategy to my repertoire, one that was inspired by physical education instructor extraordinaire and friend Andy Hair from Australia. With this idea, the kids stand behind their chair at the end of the day with their bodies in an athletic stance and their hands flat on their desktop. The goal of this game is for each child to retrieve their bag of words from inside their closed pencil box as quickly as possible and hold it up for all to see—once I give the "go" signal. When I say, "Get ready, get set, go," the kids reach for their bags and raise their hands to the sky. If, on the other hand, I borrow Andy's clever expression and say, "Get ready, get setty, eat spaghetti," the kids know not to move. I usually employ Andy's phrase a few times before uttering the real "go" signal, and I do my best to make the two commands sound identical for as long as I can. This activity sharpens listening skills, increases self-discipline, and guarantees that the kids pack their bags. I also feel good because I know I'm helping my students develop the skill of not jumping offsides if they one day grow up to become defensive linemen in football.

The next time you need your students to remember to take something home that they're not in the routine of taking home, try something a little novel and silly.

6) THINK STARTERS

An effective way to help students improve their ability to perform classroom routines is to use what educator Madeline Hunter, in her book *Discipline That Develops Self-Discipline*, calls "think starters." Imagine Randy has just handed me a paper with no name on it. If I told him, "Put your name on it," that would be a "think stopper" because I'm the one pointing out his mistake. On the other hand, imagine that I asked, "What do you need to do before handing me this paper?" In this case I'm helping Randy to discover his own mistake. That would be a think starter.

Asking instead of telling shifts the responsibility to Randy. Think starters give students ownership of their behavior. By encouraging kids to reflect on their actions, think starters help them internalize effective habits and build their capacity for the future. While Randy may have forgotten to put his name on the paper this time, think starters increase the chances that he will remember to do it next time.

7) CIRCULATE AND ENCOURAGE

"Circulate and Encourage" is a simple, non-threatening way to increase student participation in class discussions, especially with those children who tend not to raise their hands due to shyness or a lack of confidence.

Here's how it works. Imagine that I'm reading a story aloud to my students about a girl who needs to overcome a difficult obstacle to solve a problem. At the conclusion of the story, I want to highlight the different character traits the girl displays. So, I ask everyone which traits, in their opinion, helped her the most.

After posing the question, I give everyone approximately 15–30 seconds of "quiet think time." This initial step "levels the playing field" by providing all children with a chance to process the question and generate a thoughtful response. Without this "think time," faster thinkers are likely to raise their hands first and dominate the conversation, and this discourages widespread participation.

Next, I ask my students to do a pair-share, in which each child discusses the question with a neighbor. Here's where the "Circulate and Encourage" strategy comes into play.

While the kids are talking in pairs, I move around the room and listen to these conversations, paying particularly close attention to the contributions of those students who tend not to raise their hand. Assume I hear one of these children, whom we will call George, make a strong point to his partner. I compliment that idea, let George know that I think everyone else in the class would benefit from hearing it, and inform him that I will be calling on him first when our whole-group discussion starts.

After the pair-share, I bring everyone together and ask George to share his idea. Because he knows he will be chosen and has already received positive feedback for his idea, he is likely to present his thought confidently. When he does, I again compliment that idea and explain to the class why I thought everyone should hear it. George's confidence will rise, and he will be more likely to volunteer in the future because of this positive experience.

8) ACCEPTABLE VOICE INDICATOR (AVI)

At the start of the school year, it is natural for students to wonder how quiet they need to be when working at their seats. Do the kids have to be completely silent? Can they talk softly? Can they talk loudly? To address this issue, I created a chart called the Acceptable Volume Indicator, AVI for short. The AVI includes three levels of noise: conversational tone, whisper, and complete silence.

During the first week of school, I introduce the AVI to the kids, explain its purpose, model each level, and describe the types of activities for which each level will be used. Then, as the kids begin their work, we practice all three levels. Once we have practiced the levels sufficiently, the students need to know that I mean what I say. The first time students exceed the acceptable noise level, I call their attention to it. If it continues to happen, we take a few moments to discuss the issue as a class. I continue to model what I expect, hold more simulation activities, give them more opportunities to practice, and explain why it's important to adjust to each level. When students understand the purpose of a procedure or routine and see the value in it, they will commit themselves to performing it better.

Don't accept unacceptable performance. Once you do, you're sending a message, loudly and clearly, that such conduct will be tolerated. There's no room for indecisiveness or vacillating. Decide how good is good enough and stick with your decisions. Be consistent and firm. As author Philip Crosby puts it in his book *Quality Without Tears*,

> The determined ... [teacher] has no recourse except to make the same point over and over until everyone believes. The first time a deviation is agreed upon, everyone will know about it before the ink is dry. 'Oh,' people will say, 'there are some things that don't have to be right.'

If, for example, a student hands you a paper without his or her name on it, hand it back (along with a think starter). If your kids return to the room from lunch making too much noise, have them go back outside and line up again. Such actions are not punishments. They are effective responses that let your students know you mean what you say. Over time the students will rise to your expectations. By holding the group accountable early in the year, you will make the rest of the year much smoother.

9) WAYS TO EXCUSE STUDENTS

Many classroom tasks and routines can become mundane over time, and I encourage my students to help me find ways to make them more interesting. My favorite example deals with how I excuse the kids to recess. When I began my teaching career, I excused one table at a time with the standard "Table A, you may go, Table D, you may go, etc." After a few years, though, I tried another approach.

Here's how it works. First, I select a student volunteer to pick a category, such as foods, animals, or sports. Next, I ask the kids to think of their favorite item in that category. Once the kids have all done so, I start naming individual items. The children have permission to leave the room as soon as I name their item. My goal is to see if I can name the favorites of every student in the room without any clues from them. I always call the most obvious items first, such as baseball, football, and basketball if the category is favorite sport. After I name the obvious items, most of the kids leave, but there are always a few remaining. (Oftentimes, the children stay to watch even after their favorites have been called.) I then proceed to the lesser-known ones to see who else leaves. Typically, there are two or three kids left who experience great delight in knowing that I haven't called their favorite yet. The kids take great pride in their ability to stump me. (At some point, I surrender and ask them to tell me their favorite. Because the category changes each time, every child has many chances to stump me.) If I excuse my students later in the day using the same category, I try to remember the favorites of the kids who stumped me and excuse them first. Doing so sends a subtle yet powerful message that I value each child and listen closely to their ideas.

This method of excusing students takes only a minute or two, and besides being fun, it also gives us the opportunity to bond, learn more about one another, and express different aspects of our personalities. Sometimes, depending on the category, it's even educational. Above all, though, it's a way for us to generate interest where none existed before.

10) TAKE THE TEMPERATURE OF YOUR CLASSROOM

Inevitably, there will be times in our classrooms when things just seem a bit off. During these instances, for example, the typical level of focus and effort with which our students work may not be present or the kids may be having an unusually large number of arguments or problems on the playground with their peers.

In these moments it is important to remember the old adage, "As teachers, we don't teach content; we teach children." I always try to keep this idea in my mind, but I'm as guilty as anyone of forgetting it every once in a while. I may be so focused on rehearsing the steps of the math lesson I'm about to teach on a given morning that I am mentally unprepared to address the recess argument that's still bubbling over when the kids return to class after the bell.

To help myself gauge the overall focus level, morale, and mood of my students, I make it a point to check the group's "temperature" on a consistent basis.

One strategy for doing this is built into our morning routine. During this time my students and I check in with one another using a brief team-building activity from Jeanne Gibbs' terrific book *Tribes*. Using a 1–10 scale, each student states a number expressing how he or she is doing that day. (I describe this idea in detail in Part 3.) I'm always on the lookout for low numbers so that, as the day unfolds, I can offer these students comfort and cheer to boost their spirits. I encourage the kids to do the same.

If the difficulties of the class go beyond those of a small number of children, I may need to adjust the pacing, grouping arrangement, or presentation of classroom lessons and activities. I am a huge believer in cooperative learning, and my students work in pairs at least once or twice per day. If my students are having trouble working cooperatively for one reason or another, I will scale back the group work for the time being and schedule more independent work activities.

Similarly, if some students are having trouble focusing on their work at their current seats because they are distracting or distracted by peers, I will move them to a quieter, more private part of the room.

Fortunately, I do not have to make these types of adjustments frequently, but these proactive steps are often needed in the short-term until the class finds its focus, regains its momentum, and settles whatever issues it is confronting.

Checking the temperature of our classroom on a regular basis allows us to minimize disruptions, maintain morale, and maximize learning.

BIBLIOGRAPHY

Crosby, P. (1984). *Quality without Tears*. New York: McGraw-Hill.

Gibbs, J. (1995). *Tribes: A New Way of Learning and Being Together*. Sausalito, CA: Center Source Systems, LLC.

Hunter, M. (1990). *Discipline That Develops Self-Discipline*. El Segundo, CA: TIP Publications.

Reifman, S. (2008). *8 Essentials for Empowered Teaching & Learning, K–8*. Thousand Oaks, CA: Corwin Press.

Ways to Motivate and Inspire Students

11) QUOTE OF THE DAY

For over 20 years, discussing the Quote of the Day has been one of my very favorite parts of my job. Even though it's called the Quote of the Day, my students and I typically hold these talks 2–3 times a week. The exercise starts when I present the day's quote on the board. These sayings come from a variety of sources and relate to and reinforce important ideas, such as our habits of character, quality, success, and health and wellness.

After a volunteer reads the quote aloud, I give everyone a few moments of "quiet think time" to consider its meaning and relevance. Next, we do a pair-share to maximize participation in the activity, and then I call on several students to share their thoughts with the group. I conclude the activity by offering my own thoughts.

In these whole-class discussions, students may choose to identify the habit or larger idea the quote addresses, give their interpretations of the quote's meaning, or share examples demonstrating how the quote applies to their daily lives. It is important to emphasize that there are no right or wrong answers.

Though the conversations take only a few minutes, the exercise is a valuable one because it encourages kids to think deeply, reinforces the important purposes we are serving by attending school, features an uplifting tone that appeals to the best in people, and enables the group to start the day on a positive note. Further payoffs to consistent use of this activity include better student behavior, stronger work habits and social skills, improved attitudes towards school, greater enthusiasm for and increased dedication to learning, more connections made between school and students' present and future lives, and enhanced vocabulary development.

One aspect of these discussions that I have come to appreciate more and more over the years is what an incredible opportunity this exercise affords me to share inspirational stories and examples that resonate with the kids and make a deep impact on them. Some of these anecdotes come from my own life experience while others feature people my students may know and admire.

Perhaps my favorite quote to discuss comes from Harry F. Banks. It reads: "For success, attitude is equally as important as ability." After the kids share their ideas during our whole-class conversation, I love to tell the story of a middle schooler named Mike who tried out for a baseball team I coached many years ago. Eighteen kids participated in the tryouts, but my assistant and I could keep only 14 due to the capacity of the bus we drove to away games. During the tryout, the kids displayed their hitting, throwing, and other baseball skills, but it was something else that earned the star of my story his place on the team.

In batting practice Mike was playing left field as all the kids took their turn to hit. After one play the ball accidentally got past the first baseman and headed down the right field line. The right fielder should have been the one to reach the ball first and toss it back to the pitcher, but he wasn't. Instead, I saw a blur sprinting from his spot in left field across the diamond to retrieve the ball. It was Mike. I draw a picture of the field on the board as I tell this story and make a big deal about the impression Mike made on the coaching staff with his effort.

The player who was farthest from the ball was the first one to make the play—not because of speed or talent, but pure desire and hustle. Based on current skill level alone, Mike likely would not have made the team that year. It was his determination and "want to" that made the difference, and Mike ended up being an important contributor to the group.

Kids love stories like these. Not only do they humanize us, but they also convey important life lessons that children find relevant and interesting. The world around us is full of wonderful examples of inspiration, and when we make a consistent effort to find and share them, we add tremendous value to our students' lives. With our busy academic schedules, time to share inspirational stories can be difficult to find. "Quote of the Day" discussions offer the perfect forum for this endeavor, one that we can build into our morning routine 2–3 times a week.

My belief in the effectiveness of this activity to bring out the best in children, develop lasting habits, and help establish an enthusiastic, productive, team-oriented classroom culture led me to write the book *Changing Kids' Lives One Quote at a Time* so that teachers everywhere could enjoy these same benefits. This resource features 121 inspirational sayings that relate to the same ideas mentioned previously—character, quality, success, and health and wellness. From beginning to end, the quotes spiral through these topics to empower children with multiple opportunities to think about and discuss each one. Each page of the book contains an inspirational quote and a corresponding set of "talking points" that teachers and parents may choose to use for reference when discussing the quotes with children.

SAMPLE QUOTES AND TALKING POINTS

(adapted from *Changing Kids' Lives One Quote at a Time*)

Quote #1

"If you'll not settle for anything less than your best, you will be amazed at what you can accomplish in your lives."

–Vince Lombardi

Pride

- A great quote to discuss at the beginning of a new school year. Discussing this quote helps establish a culture of high expectations and lets students know that their very best effort is expected every day.
- While this idea of maintaining the highest standard of effort may begin as a classroom expectation, the goal is for students to internalize it so that it eventually becomes a personal expectation.

Quote #2

"It is better to light a candle than to complain about the darkness."

– R. Herzog

Positive Attitude

- This is another great quote to discuss at the beginning of a new school year. Discussing this quote helps your students develop a problem solving orientation and empowers students to take action when school and life's inevitable challenges arise.
- Students are more likely to solve their own problems and less likely to complain or sit helplessly once this type of problem solving orientation is established in your classroom culture.

Quote 3

"Victories that are easy are cheap. Those only are worth having which come as the result of hard work."

– Henry Ward Beecher

Perseverance

- Discussing this quote helps students understand that nothing worthwhile ever comes easily. Consistent hard work will be necessary to reach demanding goals.

- It's important for students to know that they won't be able to achieve many of their goals in a day or a week or a month; they will need to keep plugging away consistently, over time, to realize the results they are seeking.
- Sometimes working hard is interesting and exhilarating; sometimes it's not. Either way, we keep going with all our might.

Quote #4

"One hundred years from now, it will not matter what kind of car I drove, what kind of house I lived in, how much money I had in my bank account, or what my clothes looked like. But the world may be a little better because I cared enough to try to make a difference."

– Variation of a quote from Forest E. Witcraft

Service

- Discussing this quote can help students reflect on what's truly important in their lives. Of course, having money, shelter, and clothing is important, and if students want to make a lot of money and live in a big house, more power to them. Hopefully, though, they will also value service and try to make a difference in the lives of others.
- Take a minute to brainstorm with your students various types of service that they already perform or that they may wish to provide as they get older.

Quote #5

"The difference between ordinary and extraordinary is that little EXTRA!"

– Bonnie Hopper

Self-discipline

- Some students may quickly recognize the wordplay involved with this quote and notice how by adding the word "extra" to the word "ordinary," the word "extraordinary" is formed.
- The message of this quote is another that we should strive to build into the culture of our classrooms early each school year: By consistently adding that little extra effort, putting in a little extra time, and caring a little bit more about our work, we can accomplish extraordinary things in the long run.

12) YOU AND FUTURE YOU

This brief video features a story, told through a series of simple drawings, that helps kids better understand why it's so important to work hard in school and take their education seriously. This project was inspired by Dan Roam, author of the amazing book *Draw to Win*, and a New Zealand indie band called "The Beths." You can find the video on YouTube.[1] In addition to showing the video in class and discussing its main messages with my students, I email the link to parents so they can have a follow-up conversation at home.

On my "Teaching Kids" YouTube channel,[2] you can find dozens of other short videos that I've created for educators and parents.

13) "MAKING THE CHOICE" VISUAL

Because so many children are visual learners, I love creating inspirational images that resonate with kids and convey important messages in ways that text alone cannot. Whenever I design a new visual, I search for just the right images on Google. Because I don't own the copyright to these images, I'm unable to include them in this book. I provide verbal explanations only. You can find the visuals in this section on the "Teaching the Whole Child" board of my Pinterest page.[3] If you email me, I will send you a copy of the "Making the Choice" visual.

This visual is designed to encourage children to make what I call "The Choice." When kids make "The Choice," they are dedicating themselves to becoming quality students.

The visual shows how making this choice can initiate a virtuous cycle that promises wonderful academic and behavioral results. When students make the choice, they are making the decision to care more and try harder, and this leads them to produce better, higher quality work. When this happens, others take notice. Teachers will give them positive feedback. So will parents and classmates. The kids will even give themselves positive feedback as they realize they are producing better work. This causes their confidence to increase and causes them to feel prouder and more enthusiastic about school. That leads the kids to develop higher personal standards. The cycle continues as the children care more and try even harder.

This visual is especially powerful when using it with children who haven't yet made the choice, and sharing it with their parents, as I do annually at our Back to School Night. No matter how many other efforts we make to inspire children, they are all unlikely to bear fruit until the kids have first made the choice to dedicate themselves to becoming quality students.

Making "The Choice" Begins a Virtuous Cycle
The Choice: To dedicate yourself to becoming a QUALITY student

The CYCLE CONTINUES as you care even more & try even harder.

You feel PROUDER and MORE ENTHUSIASTIC about school.

You receive POSITIVE FEEDBACK (from yourself and others).

You CARE MORE & TRY HARDER in school.

You develop HIGHER PERSONAL STANDARDS.

Your CONFIDENCE increases.

You produce BETTER, HIGHER QUALITY WORK.

14) THE DRIVE FOR 5

For most of my career, two powerful sets of habits have guided the work I do with my students. Together, the Habits of Mind and Habits of Character show children the specific traits and behaviors needed to become better thinkers, better students, and better people. These 22 habits empower children to maximize their considerable potential, and I simply cannot imagine myself teaching in a classroom without using these ideas as daily reference points.

Recently, I have noticed that a few of the behaviors included among this larger list seem to have particular power in explaining why some students consistently achieve success in school and why others haven't yet been able to do so. Of course, factors that lie outside the control of teachers and schools most certainly impact how well children perform in the classroom, but the good news is that there are a small number of "high-leverage" behaviors that all children can learn and that all teachers can nurture and develop. With time, effort, and consistent attention paid to these five areas, every child can become a highly successful student and experience the greater confidence, higher self-esteem, and greater learning gains that result from this success.

I describe my quest to help children develop these behaviors as "The Drive for 5," due to the fact that the initial letters of each behavior can be combined to spell the word *drive*. On Pinterest, you will find the visuals that comprise this set.[4] One features the "drive" acronym, another provides an introduction to this construct, and the remaining five each explain one of the traits. I share this idea with students at the beginning of every school year and with families at Back to School Night. At our parent conferences in November, I give each family the "acronym" visual to place on a refrigerator or bulletin board so that these ideas remain visible and accessible throughout the year. This has been one of my most ambitious endeavors, and I believe it to be the one with the greatest potential to impact student performance. It is my hope that by giving attention to these high-leverage behaviors, we can empower all of our students to be successful in school and beyond.

Below you will find the five parts of the acronym, along with the text found in the introductory visual and five "trait" visuals.

D – Demonstrate drive and grit
R – Reach for the stars
I – Immediately ask for help when I need it
V – Visualize my future goals
E – Engage in energetic listening

Introduction: All children can be highly successful students. The key is to focus our attention in the right places. It turns out that there are five powerful steps kids can take to enjoy the greater confidence, higher self-esteem, and greater learning gains that come from being successful in school. Our quest to develop these behaviors is called "The Drive for 5."

Demonstrate drive and grit: The first step in becoming a successful student is making a commitment to education and deciding that doing well in school matters to you. Once you've done this, you are excited to arrive at school each day, and you work with energy, enthusiasm, and passion. You take responsibility for your learning and don't need reminders to focus. You are disciplined. You invest yourself completely in your work and make productive use of your time. When difficult challenges arise, you enjoy and embrace them, and you persevere until the end. How you sit while working and while listening and how you carry yourself are important parts of demonstrating drive.

Reach for the stars: Successful students hold themselves to impressively high personal standards with regard to their work, effort, and behavior. You reach this level by caring deeply about your work and not rushing through it. Your goal isn't simply to finish; it's to produce quality work. You take uncommon pride in what you do and only want to turn in work that represents your very best effort, even if it means putting in extra time. You understand that every piece of work you do is like a self-portrait. You won't settle for anything less than your best. An important part of having high personal standards is paying attention to detail while reading, answering questions, and proofreading written work.

Immediately ask for help when I need it: Successful students expect to understand new information during lessons and while reading. When they don't, it's as if an alarm bell goes off in their heads, and they immediately raise their hands to ask questions and gain clarity. They're not shy, and they don't worry that classmates will judge them. They feel comfortable speaking up for themselves without any fear or worry. After all, there's nothing to worry about. We're all in this together.

Visualize my future goals: Successful students have a strong understanding of why they're in school and why it's important to work hard and do well academically. They know that doing well in school matters, both now and in the future. These kids understand the link between today's successes and tomorrow's opportunities. They think about such things as what type of careers and passions they might want to pursue and what areas they might want to study in college. Understanding the multiple purposes of doing well in school increases motivation to learn and leads to higher levels of maturity.

Engage in energetic listening: Successful students are attentive listeners. These kids listen closely when their teachers present lessons or give important directions, and they listen just as well when their classmates are sharing information and asking and answering questions. Successful students listen closely to everyone; they don't miss a thing. You can see it in the posture they take during instructional lessons and in the eye contact they consistently make with the speaker. They want to absorb as much information as possible during lessons and discussions, and they participate frequently. They involve themselves in the conversation, enthusiastically and confidently.

15) KEYS TO VICTORY

Before the kickoff of a football game, you are likely to hear the announcers discuss each team's "keys to victory." For example, Tony Romo of CBS may describe how the New England Patriots need to run the ball effectively, protect Tom Brady so he has time to pass, and play tough defense.

In the classroom, children have their own keys to victory. Over the past few years, I've discussed this idea with my students at assessment time. Before we take an end-of-unit math assessment, for example, I ask everyone to identify the single most important thing they need to do to earn a high score. For some kids, it is paying close attention to detail. For others, it's reading the directions carefully, making sure they show all their work, or checking their work thoroughly at the end.

Once the kids have each identified their individual key to victory, I encourage them to write or sketch that idea at the top of their papers before they begin working. That visual reminder has made a significant difference for many students, providing a quick, simple form of motivation and inspiration. Plus, this process helps children understand themselves better as learners and promotes reflective thinking. My students and I establish several class symbols throughout the year, and many kids like to sketch one of these at the top of their papers. Others create their own.

16) TOWER OF OPPORTUNITY FOLDOUT

The Tower of Opportunity is a four-sided, seven-story structure that my architect friend helped me create several years ago to serve as a powerful visual metaphor for children about the importance of doing well in school. The Tower provides a tangible, novel way for teachers to help kids better understand the purposes of their learning, find meaning in their work, and connect what they are learning in school to their goals for the future.

Each floor of the Tower features one of the seven "life roles" that Dale Parnell defines in his terrific book *Why Do I Have to Learn This?* Each role (e.g., Citizen, Lifelong Learner, Worker) connects to a set of responsibilities that all individuals occupy in their lives. The role names occupy one side of the tower while specific examples of each role occupy the other three. The examples of each role are printed on doors that include tiny doorknobs. The design of the tower allows us, as teachers, to convey the message that life is rich with opportunities, choices, and options, and that in order to take advantage of these opportunities, maximize our choices, and give ourselves the greatest number of options, we need an education. Put simply, education is the key that opens doors. The harder we work in school and the more we learn, the more doors we can open for ourselves.

Every week or two, as part of our morning routine, my students and I focus on a specific aspect of the Tower and discuss how what we are learning in class connects in some way to our goals for the future. Every time we do, I am able to remind students of the numerous ways in which their learning can be put to use and the numerous reasons why learning matters so much. When teachers use the Tower with students, we expand their perspective and encourage them to think beyond their present reality. Furthermore, we provide them with a glimpse of what a productive, well-rounded life can look like.

In addition to these scheduled discussions, the structure was designed to be used as a significant reference point that teachers and students revisit frequently. Sometimes conversations involving the Tower can occur spontaneously—at the start of a new unit or project, for example, or when we choose to discuss an item we heard on the news, share a personal story, or try to capitalize on a learnable moment. The goal is for the Tower to maintain a consistent presence in the classroom throughout the year.

Though I haven't yet found a way to make this structure available to fellow teachers, I have created a complete template of the Tower's four sides, from which you can make copies for your students, fold the sides into a freestanding replica, or design a larger model for your classroom. You can find pictures of two of the Tower's four sides on my website,[5] or on Pinterest.[6] If you would like to receive a copy of the template, please email me.

Here are some specific topics you may wish to discuss during your "Tower Talks."

- Tower introduction: I provide a brief introduction and overview of each role and focus on one role per discussion for our first seven talks.
- Arrangement of floors: I explain the bottom-to-top sequence of roles. While the potential certainly exists for people assuming any role to make a difference in the lives of others, the roles located on the bottom tend to focus primarily on individual needs, goals, and priorities, while those higher on the Tower tend to involve progressively larger numbers of people. I'm the first to concede that this order is rough at best, but I believe it benefits children to arrange the roles in this manner to highlight the idea of service. As long as we discuss the inexactness of the sequence with students so that they don't view the order as being overly rigid, there shouldn't be any problem.
- "Zooming in": I focus on specific floors or doors that may hold special significance at a given time. During an election year, for example, conversations can center on the role of citizens. Specifically, teachers and students can discuss candidates, issues, voting procedures, and how education and the importance of an education connect to them. If we don't have time in our schedules for a full elections unit, we can use "Tower Time" for brief discussions, presentations, and sharing of information and opinions.
- Learning connections: The students and I connect what we are currently learning in class to future goals or larger purposes.
- Open forum: Periodically, I have the students pick a role or door and connect it to something currently happening at school or in their lives outside of school.

- <u>Upcoming events</u>: The Tower can offer a useful framework when mentioning upcoming local events (e.g., The Los Angeles Times Festival of Books) or institutions (e.g., museums, libraries) that connect to one or more roles.
- <u>Articles</u>: Information found in newspaper or magazine articles can tie in well with the emphases of the Tower. For example, every year I share an article describing a study that compares the cumulative earnings, life expectancies, and health of people who graduate from high school with those of individuals who don't. Very powerful.
- <u>"A glimpse of the future" discussions</u>: Teachers select a role and students share their goals or plans related to that role. For example, if I select the role of Lifelong Learner, students can share a college they hope to attend or an academic area they wish to pursue. If I select the role of Worker, kids can share the types of jobs they might want one day. If we are discussing the role of Family Member and Friend or Citizen, the children can talk about the contributions they want to make to their families and communities.

17) INSPIRATIONAL READ ALOUDS

One terrific way to inspire children is to read aloud stories in which the main characters achieve success by committing themselves to education, demonstrating strong character, and overcoming obstacles. In his book *Crash Course*, entrepreneur Chris Whittle supports this idea when he advocates "methodically exposing children to greatness, excellence, success in many fields and then emphasizing how learning was important to each example. Every day every school should put excellence on display."

What's particularly important is to select a wide variety of individuals so that students everywhere can identify with at least a few whose life stories resonate with *their* life stories and whose backgrounds resemble their own. For children who believe that attending school and earning an education cannot make a difference for people like themselves, our choices need to provide abundant, inspiring examples that prove otherwise.

Whittle's powerful message about helping children see the usefulness of education inspired me to write the book *2-Minute Biographies for Kids*. The resource contains 1-page biographies of 19 well-known individuals who used education to make better lives for themselves. The biographies trace the learning paths of the featured men and women and emphasize the educational accomplishments that made their later success possible. The stories also highlight the adversity these people faced, the obstacles they overcame, and the positive character traits they demonstrated. In addition, interesting facts, anecdotes, and quotes are included so children understand that these individuals were at one time kids just like themselves.

The individuals included in this book were chosen with great care. Collectively, they form a distinguished group, featuring pioneers who broke barriers and gained entry into fields where access had previously been denied, significant racial and ethnic diversity, multiple educational routes to success, a variety of career paths and occupational fields, and examples from different periods in history.

2-Minute Biographies for Kids is an advertisement for education. The book's primary goal is to encourage children everywhere to become more determined, more motivated, more purposeful learners. The idea is that once children understand the critical role that education played in empowering these people to achieve the greatness for which they are known today, they will work harder and be more likely to persevere through difficult times.

In each story the featured individual is not initially identified, thus creating an engaging "riddle" scenario. As kids listen to the title and the biography, they are learning about the person's life story, and they are also attempting to determine the identity of the individual being described. The final sentence of each biography reveals the person's name.

You may want to stop before reading this concluding sentence and ask the children in your audience if they would like to guess the individual's identity. Once the identity is revealed, you can then engage children in a brief discussion in which interesting and important aspects of the person's life are highlighted and potential lessons learned are emphasized. Below and on Routledge.com, you will find a sample biography from the book.

> **SAMPLE BIOGRAPHY FROM *2-MINUTE*
> *BIOGRAPHIES FOR KIDS***

She Learned Early in Life to Shoot for the Stars

As a child, she had always been fascinated by planets, stars, and galaxies, but never did she dream of becoming a scientist. She was born in Los Angeles, CA on May 26, 1951, to parents who deeply valued education. Her father Dale was a political science professor at Santa Monica College; her mom was a teacher and voracious reader. In their book *Shooting for the Stars*, authors Jane and Sue Hurwitz remark that she and her younger sister Karen "were raised in an atmosphere that encouraged individual exploration. Accordingly, {she} believed that she could undertake any activity that she felt capable of or wished to learn about. Being a girl never prevented her from doing anything she wanted." She loved to read Nancy Drew mysteries, James Bond spy novels, and a fair amount of science fiction. Looking back now, it is fitting that one of her heroes was Superman.

She developed an intense passion for both science and sports. By age five, she was reading the sports section of the newspaper and memorizing baseball statistics. There was even a time when she dreamed of playing for the hometown Dodgers. She was so good at softball and football that she was often the only girl selected to play in neighborhood games with boys. From these games, she learned two critical lessons: the importance of being a team player and that girls can compete in games with boys.

As she grew up, major changes were occurring in the field of space exploration. The Soviet Union had taken the lead over the U.S. in the "Space Race" by launching the first artificial satellite to orbit the earth in 1957 and by sending the first person into space in 1961. Along with thousands of Americans, her interest in space increased during this time. Tennis soon became her main sport, and her talent, motivation, determination, and perseverance helped her become a top junior player. In 1964, she won a partial scholarship to the all-girls Westlake School, where she met Dr. Elizabeth Mommaerts, a teacher who encouraged her to become a scientist. In high school she continued to progress with her tennis while also studying chemistry, physics, trigonometry, and calculus. After graduation, she attended Swarthmore College, a small liberal arts college just outside Philadelphia, where for two years she excelled at tennis. She then came home so she could play all year round in the warmer climate.

Eventually, she concluded that she didn't quite have what it took to become a pro tennis player, so she dedicated herself to becoming a scientist. She went to Stanford University and in 1973 graduated with degrees in English and physics. In the years that followed, she earned her master's degree and Ph. D in astrophysics, the study of the physical and chemical characteristics of matter in space. In 1977, unsure of what kind of job to get, she came across an advertisement in the university newspaper. NASA was looking for mission specialists to conduct experiments on board the space shuttle, and for the first time women were urged to apply.

Even though there were more than 8,000 applicants for the program, she made it, due to the combination of her science background, athletic ability, scholastic achievement, and reputation as a team player. On June 18, 1983, she served as mission specialist on the space shuttle *Challenger*. With a crowd estimated at 250,000 watching from Kennedy Space Center, she became America's first female astronaut and the youngest American to take part in a space mission. Her participation wasn't simply an outstanding personal achievement; it would help create new opportunities for other American women in a variety of professions. Her courage and commitment to working as part of a team earned her the respect of fellow astronauts, the admiration of millions of Americans, and a place in history. Her name ... is Dr. Sally Ride.

18) "TUG-OF-WAR" VISUAL

Children commonly have two conflicting goals in mind while they are working. First, they want to do a great job. Second, they want to be done. Throughout the year, I emphasize to my students that quality is always the most important priority, and we need to be willing to take our time, focus on the task at hand, and put forth our very best effort if we wish to be successful in school and in life.

I have discussed this "tug-of-war" concept with my class for several years, and I created a visual that shows a boy in the center working on a task with thinking bubbles extending out from both the left side and right side of his head. The bubble on the left side represents the "I just want to finish" approach; the bubble on the right, the "I want to make it great" approach. The image resonates with children and serves as an effective conversation starter.

Discussing the visual[7] furthers our efforts to help students develop higher personal standards of quality with their schoolwork. Many kids tend to race through their work, pay little attention to its quality, and want only to get it done. When we rush, quality suffers, and children need to know that. The "tug-of-war" visual shines a spotlight on this issue and points out that while working on a task, we face an important decision. Do we just want to finish, or do we want to make it great? Do we want to complete the task as quickly as possible, or are we willing to slow down and invest the necessary time and effort to create something that makes us proud?

19) INTRINSIC MOTIVATION CHART

In *Punished by Rewards* Alfie Kohn describes the relationship between extrinsic and intrinsic motivation. Rewards and punishments are both examples of extrinsic motivation. I define extrinsic motivation to mean that *an individual desires to engage in a task not because of any connection to the task itself, but because of outside incentives.* (In fact, the Latin prefix "ex" means "out of.") For example, if I begin listening to a certain radio station only because it's giving away $10,000 to caller 12, then I am extrinsically motivated. I'm not listening to the station because I enjoy the music it plays or the personality of the DJs. My desire to engage in the task of listening has nothing to do with the act of listening itself; I listen so that I can win money. I listen, not for its own sake, but because it is a stepping-stone to a greater good. Listening is simply a means to an end.

In contrast, intrinsic motivation focuses on what lies within the task, not on what successful completion of the task will earn. By intrinsically motivated, I mean that *an individual desires to engage in a task due to the nature of the task itself or because of something inherent in the task.* For example, I was initially attracted to the sport of paddle tennis as a young child because I enjoyed running around, hitting the ball, and planning strategy. I began playing the game for its own sake, not for extrinsic incentives such as prize money. For any task, whether it's playing a sport or solving a math problem, intrinsic motivation exists when one or more of the following conditions apply:

- I find the task interesting.
- I find meaning in it.
- The task is important to me.
- I feel a sense of mastery or accomplishment when I do it well.
- I enjoy the challenge the task provides.
- I take personal pride and satisfaction in doing the task well.
- I value the learning opportunity the task offers.
- The task offers opportunities for self-expression and creativity.

Kohn cites research demonstrating that extrinsic motivation destroys intrinsic motivation. Though many popular classroom management approaches rely on table points, marble jars, and other systems rooted in extrinsic motivation, these methods present a variety of serious problems. Further discussion of this topic lies outside the scope of this book, but in my view, this is one of the most important topics educators need to consider when developing their teaching philosophies. You can find more information about this topic in my book *8 Essentials for Empowered Teaching & Learning, K–8.*

Introducing the aforementioned bullet points to your students at the beginning of each school year and referring to them in the months that follow encourages everyone to find interest, meaning, and joy in their learning and helps children develop wonderful habits that will serve them well for a lifetime.

20) CLASS MISSION STATEMENT VISUAL

During the first full week of each school year, my students and I write our class mission statement to establish a sense of purpose; set a high expectation level for our work, effort, and behavior; and describe who we are and who we'd like to become. I describe this four-day process in detail in both my ebook *The First 10 Minutes: A Classroom Morning Routine that Reaches and Teaches the Whole Child* and a TeachersPayTeachers item entitled "The Class Mission Statement Starter Kit."

This past year, after reading Dan Roam's terrific book *Draw to Win* over the summer, I also had my students create a visual to represent the statement's main ideas. The rationale behind making the companion visual is that seeing the statement as an image may help students understand the ideas on a deeper level, and the ideas may resonate with the kids in a way they might not with text alone.

The students all had the opportunity to contribute to the process of creating the visual, and one student made our final draft using Google Draw. To keep these ideas in mind throughout the year, we put the image on one of our classroom doors and on the front of our class t-shirt.

While the process of writing a class mission statement may not necessarily be something you can implement tomorrow, creating a class visual is. Though my students and I use the visual as a complement to our class mission statement, it can also serve as a stand-alone effort to establish purpose, set an expectation level, and describe the kind of environment you and your kids would like to build. In fact, I recommend creating this type of image if you work with different groups of children throughout the day and don't have the time to write a mission statement with each group or if you're well into your school year and would like to try out this process with an eye toward writing a class mission statement at the start of the next school year.

To begin the process of creating a visual with your students, either start from scratch or use the one shown below as a starting point. Your students may have a clearer idea of what you're asking them to design if they can see what another class has already done. Orally or in writing, have the children answer questions such as the ones shown below. The answers will inform the specific parts you decide to include in the visual. Next, create a draft of the image or have one or more kids take responsibility for the draft and then revise it as a class until you are satisfied with it.

- What are our most important class goals this year?
- What are our highest learning priorities this year?
- What ideas distinguish us as a unique group of people with a unique sense of purpose?
- What type of environment do we want to create together?
- What are we determined to accomplish together?
- How will we know when we are being a successful class?

Here is a description of the various parts of the class visual my students and I created. If you'd prefer to show your kids a short video of me talking about the image, you can find it on YouTube.[8]

Let's begin on the bottom left. The image of the sun rising reminds all of us that every day is a new opportunity to do some great learning. No matter what might have happened the day before, each day offers a fresh start.

In many ways our school year can be viewed as a quest to improve continuously and level up. Throughout my career, I have emphasized a "teaching the whole child" approach, and "leveling up" is a concept that we can apply to each academic area, our Habits of Mind and Habits of Character, even to our friendships and our health and wellness.

Leveling up is the idea that the two kids moving up the stairs represent. It's important to note that they're not walking up the stairs; they are charging. They're bringing energy, determination, and passion to their learning. That's what the lightning bolt on the left conveys.

As each of us commits to continuous improvement, we don't go at it alone. There's a strong sense of teamwork, kindness, and cooperation in the class. That's why the two kids are reaching for each other's hands. As we try to improve individually, we're also trying to help others level up.

The battery near the top step also relates to the impact we can all have on one another. A term we frequently use in class is "battery charger," a person whose sheer presence makes the classroom environment better and happier because of the positive spirit they consistently display.

Above the head of each child, you see light bulbs that show how we're all bright, talented people with amazing potential.

One thing that's different about each child is their expression. On the left, the smiling face is designed to show that learning should feel good and that our classroom experiences should be joyful. Furthermore, the smile means that we're confident, enthusiastic students who are engaged and intrinsically motivated.

On the figure on the right, the expression and beads of sweat show that sometimes things can be difficult, and doing our work can be a grind. When this happens, we don't shy away from it. We embrace challenges and demonstrate perseverance and grit.

Finally, the "HQ" in the top right corner connects to our expectations. Specifically, it expresses that we always work for the highest quality and that we won't settle for less than our best.

NOTES

1 https://www.youtube.com/watch?v=RkmE7mkeJsl
2 https://www.youtube.com/channel/UC78IiitPf4na_kvo6QbUlMw
3 https://www.pinterest.com/stevereifman/teaching-the-whole-child/
4 https://www.pinterest.com/stevereifman/the-drive-for-5/
5 http://stevereifman.com/teaching-books/tower-of-opportunity
6 https://www.pinterest.com/stevereifman/teaching-the-whole-child
7 https://www.pinterest.com/pin/401524123001310969/
8 https://www.youtube.com/watch?v=4qzO5L9QrlY

BIBLIOGRAPHY

Kohn, A. (1993). *Punished by Rewards*. New York: Houghton Mifflin.

Parnell, D. (1995). *Why Do I Have to Learn This?* Waco, TX: CORD Communications.

Reifman, S. (2008). *8 Essentials for Empowered Teaching & Learning, K–8*. Thousand Oaks, CA: Corwin Press.

Reifman, S. (2012). *Changing Kids Lives One Quote at a Time*. Morrisville, NC: Lulu Press.

Reifman, S. (2013). *2-Minute Biographies for Kids*. Santa Monica, CA: Author.

Reifman, S. (2013). *The First 10 Minutes: A Classroom Morning Routine That Reaches and Teaches the Whole Child*. Santa Monica, CA: Author.

Roam, D. (2016). *Draw to Win*. New York: Penguin Random House LLC.

Whittle, C. (2005). *Crash Course*. New York: Riverhead Books.

Ways to Personalize Learning

21) PASSION SURVEY

When I first administered the Passion Survey several years ago, I knew right away I would use this activity every fall during the first week of school. It was educational love at first sight. The survey is simply a piece of paper on which students list their four favorite hobbies and activities and then draw themselves pursuing these passions.

At the top of the sheet, I include the following introduction. On the paper you distribute, feel free to include a similar opening that reflects your passions.

> I absolutely love football. I could watch it and talk about it all day long and then look forward to doing it all over again the next day. I also love music, working out, reading, and writing. These are some of my **passions**. Passions are hobbies and activities that we love. They are our favorite things to do, talk about, and think about. Passions are what we would do all day long if we could, and we would never get bored or tired of them. Passions are what we like spending time doing when nobody is asking us to do something else.

Once everyone finishes, I take the papers home to create a chart displaying the results. (If the class, as a whole, names more passions than the top of the chart can accommodate, I combine topics or create larger categories and then use letter codes to identify each child's specific passions. For example, in the "Art" section of the chart, "D" stands for "Drawing," "P" for "Painting," and "A" for overall "Art.") After sharing and discussing the chart with the children, I display it prominently on one of the closet doors for the rest of the year. You can find an example of this chart on Pinterest[1]

The Passion Survey is perfect for the first week of school because it's simple and engaging, and because its results are so powerful. Specifically, this activity produces three wonderful outcomes. First, when students have the opportunity to make curricular choices, the passions provide a concrete starting point. For example, if I am stuck trying to find a topic for my information book during Writing Workshop, I can think about my passions and choose one to spark an idea. Since I love the Los Angeles Dodgers, I can write my book about the team. Motivation, interest, and productivity increase substantially when I am able to choose my topic, and they increase even more when I pick one about which I am passionate. Originally, this was the main reason I decided to give the survey—as an aid that would help students personalize the choices they make about their academic learning.

In addition, a tremendous amount of group bonding and team building occur when students discover their classmates' passions. In fact, many friendships form or strengthen because of the shared interests that children identify. Sometimes kids have been in the same class for many years and are only now learning about their shared love of certain topics or activities. After looking at the chart together, many children have even scheduled after-school playdates to pursue their common passions. This type of bonding is particularly valuable for children who are new to the school or who, in the past, have had difficulty forming friendships.

Finally, the simple fact that, as a class, we are thinking and talking and writing about our passions sends the message that it is cool to be passionate about things. Students who may not yet have found their passions will become more encouraged to look, especially when they see their classmates excited by their own passions. In addition, people tend to be happiest when they are pursuing their favorite interests, and if your students have regular opportunities to incorporate their passions into their schoolwork, your classroom will naturally become a happier, more productive place.

Taken together, the benefits of the Passion Survey have a terrific effect on the overall classroom environment and on the culture I try hard to create at the beginning of each school year. Thinking about the topics we love the most, making new friends, and demonstrating enthusiasm and excitement for our learning bring out the best in everyone and help us get our year off to a great start.

22) STUDENT LEADER

The next two ideas put a smile on the faces of all children, yet they particularly benefit those quiet, shy kids who tend to fly under the radar. The primary appeal of these ideas is simple—both guarantee that every learner receives a highly personalized form of individual attention that's 100% positive. The first affords each child the chance to become Student Leader. (This position is commonly known as "Student of the Week," but I prefer the term Student Leader because of the leadership opportunities and responsibilities I have built into the role.)

Every Friday before recess, I draw a popsicle stick from the cup I keep on the chalk tray, and the person whose name is chosen becomes Student Leader for the following week. That child gets to answer the phone, take the attendance sheet to the office, deliver things to other classes, and handle a variety of classroom monitor jobs. Each morning that child stands outside the door and greets the rest of the kids as they enter the room. In addition, (s)he leads everybody in the Pledge of Allegiance and our morning movement warmup routine. I also fill out a colorful certificate and hang it on a bulletin board where the kids can put up pictures of their family and friends and share the photos at the end of their week.

A few years ago, my students and I added a new twist to this weekly feature when I selected Tracy's name from the cup. I can get a bit silly before recess, and I joked that as a tribute to our new Student Leader, everybody needed to show up on Monday wearing a flower in their hair as Tracy routinely did. I completely forget about my little joke and was shocked when six kids showed up on Monday with flowers in their hair. Tracy was absolutely beaming when she saw this, and a new tradition was born.

The following week, a boy named Danny became Student Leader. Because he didn't routinely wear a flower in his hair, we needed a different way to honor him during his special week. He said that he liked wearing blue shirts to school, so the following week, many kids wore blue shirts to school. These tributes, which began as a throw-away joke before recess, have become a quick, simple, and powerful way to give kids their moment in the sun and make them feel like an important part of the team.

23) GIVE ALL YOUR STUDENTS THEIR OWN "THING"

Beyond offering each child a turn as Student Leader, we can personalize everyone's classroom experience and guarantee positive attention by giving learners their own *thing*. I know that's not the most elegant or precise word choice, but I'm intentionally employing a vague term because, in this section, *thing* can mean so many different, well, things. When we give kids their own thing, it can be a nickname, a job, a gesture, a signal, or a private joke—anything that makes a child feel special and acknowledged as an individual. The goal is for every child to have or be known for something that is uniquely theirs.

Typically, these examples are lighthearted and playful, yet they have the potential to produce incredibly powerful bonding moments—between teacher and student or among the whole team. Frequently, my interactions with children regarding these *things* are the best parts of my day because they're so much fun.

Let me share a few examples with you. One of Tracy's classmates was a terrific young man named Bobby. He has a heart of gold and a strong desire to do well academically. Once or twice a day, however, he would lose focus during independent work time and rest his head on his desk. When this happened, I whispered his name from my chair in the front of the room, and he would look my way. I then pretended to throw him an energy bar that he would pretend to catch and eat. That's all he needed to return to work. Besides being a bit silly, this strategy follows the effective management practice of intervening only as much as necessary when children stray off task. Eating virtual energy bars in class became Bobby's thing.

Second, on most days, before our morning circle time, I ask the children to stand behind their desks with the previous night's homework in front of them. (Usually, the kids turn in a math activity plus one other piece of written work.) To ensure that the students put their names on their papers, I have everyone point to the top of both pages. Until that year, every time we did this, the kids would extend their arms straight out in front of them and touch the top of the paper on the left with their left hand and the sheet on their right with their right hand. All that changed one day when a girl we'll call Cindy touched the sheet on the left with her right hand and the paper on the right with her left hand. This innovative maneuver soon became known as the Cindy Tuttle Cross-Handed Grip (patent pending). Other kids, with Cindy's permission, soon adopted it. This independent thinker was proud that her idea was spreading throughout the classroom, and the cross-handed grip became Cindy's thing.

These *things* can be especially valuable with children who experience daily difficulties with behavior and whose conduct can sometimes frustrate us. Focusing on something positive, such as a nickname, can lighten the mood, change the way we interact with that child, and, ultimately, change the outcome of those interactions. One year, a girl who sat in the front row of the rug during instructional lessons often lacked energy and drifted off while I was talking. I wanted to find her a nickname that captured the spirit of the active approach I was encouraging her to develop. With her permission, I began to call her Spark. This nickname didn't completely solve her difficulties, but it definitely helped her perform better. During those times when she had trouble, the nickname kept the tone positive. After all, it's hard to be frustrated with someone when you're calling them Spark.

Sometimes, a nickname or gesture will have only short-term effectiveness; other times, it can last the whole year and beyond. With regard to the former, Tracy (with the flower in her hair) was on a roll one morning. Everything she did was 100% correct. During math, I remarked, "Tracy, you really nailed that problem." When it happened again a short time later, I repeated that phrase. After a while, I said, "Tracy, we should call you the Hammer, because you're nailing everything." She laughed, and that became her nickname—for another hour or so. I initially liked the name because it was so preposterous, so *not* who she was, but it turned out that the idea of a little girl with a flower in her hair being named after a construction tool just didn't have staying power.

One idea that did stand the test of time originated approximately twenty years ago, and it's my all-time favorite example of giving kids their thing. Early in the school year, I noticed that a girl named Sara Evans always seemed to be smiling. After a while, I started calling her Smiley. (Not as original as the Hammer, I know, but it seemed to do the trick.) Fifteen years later, I was at a doctor's office talking with a young assistant who mentioned that she went to high school not far from where I taught. I started throwing out a few names to see if she might have known any of my former students. When I asked if she knew Sara Evans, she replied, "Oh, you mean Smiley?"

24) PERSONALIZED MOTIVATIONAL VISUALS

One of the most difficult challenges teachers face involves motivating students who haven't yet committed themselves fully to academic pursuits, who may never before have had positive experiences in school, and who may not yet demonstrate the drive and work ethic required to be successful. Throughout my career I have incorporated "Quote of the Day" discussions into our morning routine and used storytelling to help motivate children, and these efforts have had a significant impact on how students perform in the classroom. With some kids, however, we need to take additional action due to the severity of their situations.

Recently, I started creating personalized, inspirational visuals for some of my students. When I decided to make the first one for a child who was having an extremely difficult start to the year, I knew that his favorite football player was Seattle Seahawks running back Marshawn Lynch. Normally tough to tackle, Lynch frequently took his game to the next level and got into what's known as "Beast Mode," in which he was nearly impossible to bring down. I thought "Beast Mode" would be a perfect new nickname for this child, as it exemplified the active, determined, unstoppable mindset I was trying to help him adopt as a student.

Creating the visual was a lot of fun and didn't take that long. After finding images of the Seahawks logo, Lynch, and our team name (THQ) on Google, I located a photo of my student, at his best, working at his desk. A sample of this visual is available on Pinterest.[2]

I was eager to present the visual to him the next morning in class. I didn't know how he would react when seeing it for the first time. He was usually very quiet and tended not to show any emotion. Right away, I noticed two things. Anytime he worked in a different part of the classroom, he brought the visual with him and put it on the table next to his work. That continued until the end of the year. Second, at the end of each class period and each day, the visual was always on the top middle section of his desk. Typically, to put it kindly, neatness wasn't this child's highest priority. Papers were often lost or seen falling out of his desk and backpack. But the visual was always respected and cared for.

Whenever he did a great job focusing on his work and using his time well, he was in his version of "Beast Mode." I loved capturing these moments by calling him by his new nickname and recognizing his fine effort. Will the visual and nickname, by themselves, lead to dramatic changes and make his difficulties disappear? Of course not. But, might having something positive to look at each day that shows him at his best and on equal footing with his favorite athlete begin to make a difference for him and help him start to view school and himself more favorably? That is my sincere hope.

Shortly after I presented the visual to this student, his best friend in class asked me to make one for him. This second child also experienced great difficulty with his learning, and I was thrilled that he took the initiative and requested a visual. Unlike his buddy Beast Mode, he didn't follow sports closely and didn't have a favorite player. He said he liked the Oakland Raiders, though, so I found a picture of Derek Carr, their quarterback. Instead of the words "Beast Mode," the boy suggested that we use "Touchdown," the idea being that any time he did a great job in class, it was like he was scoring a "learning touchdown." This visual, like that of his friend, could always be found neatly arranged on his desk at the end of each school day.

Students can also create their own desktop displays and receive a boost of inspiration by placing small flat items on the top corners of their tables. One child recently wanted to put a picture of his dog on his desk because when he looked at it, the photo put him in a good mood and reduced the feelings of stress he often experienced in school. As long as kids don't become distracted by a given item, they can gain significant emotional benefits that can lead to improved focus and better academic performance.

25) VISUAL REMINDER CARDS

Conferring with students one-on-one to help them improve specific aspects of their learning is one of the most powerful instructional strategies we have at our disposal. Over the years, the work of Lucy Calkins and the Teachers College at Columbia University has highlighted the importance of frequent conferring with young readers and writers, and these private conversations pay similar dividends in math and other academic areas. Whether our goal involves reading with greater expression, beginning our writing pieces with an interesting lead, or solving multi-step word problems, conferring is a terrific way to personalize our strategy work for the benefit of each child.

Follow-up is typically the primary challenge with conferring. For example, a student, during our reading conference, may do a fantastic job of making a thoughtful prediction before starting a new chapter, yet transferring that skill to her daily reading, where it matters most, may not come as easily.

To help facilitate stronger transfer, we can use simple tools called visual reminder cards. Each card is a small, index card-sized sheet that contains the name of a specific strategy, a corresponding image, and a brief definition or description of the strategy. At the end of a conference, I like to present students with a visual reminder card focused on the strategy we just practiced. The kids then take the card back to their seats and keep it on their desks as a quick, easy reference. Seeing the card in front of them as they work significantly increases the likelihood that students will use the strategy we discussed. In addition, when the kids are all displaying their cards in this manner, it allows me to circulate throughout the room and know instantly which strategies to reinforce.

You can find a sample reminder card related to the strategy of envisioning on Pinterest. (If you're interested in the full set of 29 cards that I made to help children improve their reading, email me, and I'll send it to you.) You may decide that you'd like to create your own cards for math, writing, other subjects, and even for issues of student behavior. Over time, as you conduct more and more conferences and your students accumulate multiple cards, you can punch holes in the corner and keep the set on a small ring. With so many students practicing so many different strategies, visual reminder cards offer an effective, user-friendly way to provide the personalized support our students need.

26) UPDATES

During my teacher training program at UCLA, I enjoyed learning several engaging "sponge" activities that students could complete at their desks as they entered the room either first thing in the morning or after a break. "Updates" is my currently my favorite sponge activity, but it's not something children do independently at their seats. Rather, updates are brief whole-class conversations that occur right after lunch when we are gathering on the rug to begin our next lesson or after students pack up to go home at the end of the day before read aloud. When giving an update, kids may share anything meaningful that's happening in their lives outside of class. Popular topics include pets, athletic events, family visits, movies, and trips. I share updates, as well. Providing team members with this opportunity is a wonderful way for all of us to learn more about one another and bond. At the beginning of the year, I caution everyone to avoid sharing information about private family business, parties to which everyone in the class may not have been invited, or anything that may come across as bragging, such as getting expensive new shoes. We don't anyone feeling left out. Because kids love giving and hearing updates, they tend to carry out their transitions and come to the rug quickly, affording us more time for the activity that follows. If you want to be even cooler in the eyes of your students, refer to this activity as "S'updates" so the kids can tell everyone what's up.

27) ENTHUSIASM SURVEY

The Enthusiasm Survey has been a first-week-of-school fixture in my classroom since the mid-1990s when I read about the pioneering work being done by the Enterprise School District in Redding, California. In his book *Improving Student Learning*, then Enterprise Superintendent Lee Jenkins describes a yearly attitude survey the district conducted, in which students in grades kindergarten through eight expressed their feelings about each subject they studied. A happy face meant students liked a subject, a neutral face meant ambivalence, and a sad face meant the students disliked a subject.

The data that Enterprise collected enabled district staff to compare the percentage of happy faces by grade level for each year of the survey. In *Improving Student Learning*, Jenkins presents a graph showing a slow, gradual loss of enthusiasm that begins when students are in kindergarten and continues every year thereafter. Jenkins comments that "the data clearly show that each grade level contributed to the loss of enthusiasm." To heighten awareness of this decline, Jenkins makes the point that if 30 kindergartners enter school together, and two children per year lose their enthusiasm for learning, then only a handful would still be enthusiastic as they finish high school.

Jenkins believes that teachers are responsible for both learning and enthusiasm. He considers student enthusiasm to be an invaluable asset that educators must cherish. Students who have lost their enthusiasm for learning are less motivated to learn, less likely to put their learning to use in creative ways, and more likely to cause discipline problems. Jenkins contends that typical kindergartners have enough enthusiasm to last a lifetime, but they don't yet have the knowledge and skills they will need to be successful. Educators, he stresses, must guard this enthusiasm and protect it throughout a child's academic career. It is a school's most precious resource.

The results of the yearly attitude survey, along with other contributing forces, led Enterprise to create something called an aim, which is the overall objective that students and staff work together to accomplish. Creating an aim is an incredibly powerful way to establish a sense of purpose, drive decisions, and determine goals, but treatment of this topic lies outside the scope of this book. If you're interested in more information about how to create a classroom aim and use it to achieve maximum impact, check out *8 Essentials for Empowered Teaching and Learning, K–8* or *The First Month of School*.

My focus in this section is the survey itself. Asking children two to three times per year to indicate the subjects they enjoy, the ones they think are just OK, and the ones they don't enjoy yields valuable information. One thing that typically goes unnoticed in the classroom is that every time we introduce a new academic activity, such as a math lesson or a science investigation, students have an emotional reaction to it. As educators, we almost never notice these reactions because children are very good at keeping them hidden. Whether children like a given subject and feel confident in that area matters tremendously, as these feelings will exert an enormous influence on students' motivation, productivity, and willingness to put forth sustained effort.

Encouraging our students to become more enthusiastic about the subjects they study in school is an important priority, and our efforts will pay dividends in both the short-run and long-run. As I mentioned in the previous paragraph, students who enjoy a subject are more likely to work harder on every activity in that area, produce higher quality work, and persevere when they encounter difficulty. In the long-run, student enthusiasm will lead to greater intellectual curiosity, creativity, openness to new ideas, and the desire to learn more and more. Children who work with enthusiasm become lifelong learners.

The data collected during the first week about each individual child and about the class as a whole provide us with our starting point. Jenkins notes that the initial data are neither good nor bad; they simply represent where we are as a class when the kids first walk through our doors. From there, we talk with the group throughout the year about ways we can make our learning more enjoyable, implement these suggestions, and assess our progress when we conduct our next survey. In addition, we can meet with students one-on-one to offer encouragement when they're having a difficult time with subjects that they don't yet enjoy, point out aspects of certain academic areas they might find interesting, or share stories of times when we were kids and didn't really like a subject but hung in there and discovered something that changed our view.

I'm a big believer in the theory that says people tend to like what they're good at, and over the years I have seen a definite correlation between children's proficiency in a given academic area and their enthusiasm for it. So, while these class discussions and individual conversations play an important role in helping children become more enthusiastic about their learning, nothing boosts enthusiasm like consistent diligence and steady academic improvement.

NOTES

1   https://www.pinterest.com/stevereifman/teaching-the-whole-child
2   https://www.pinterest.com/stevereifman/teaching-the-whole-child

BIBLIOGRAPHY

Jenkins, L. (1997). *Improving Student Learning: Applying Deming's Quality Principles in Classrooms.* Milwaukee, WI: ASQC Quality Press.

Reifman, S. (2008). *8 Essentials for Empowered Teaching & Learning, K–8.* Thousand Oaks, CA: Corwin Press.

Reifman, S. (2014). *The First Month of School.* Santa Monica, CA: Author.

Reifman, S. (2016). *1/2 Ways to Personalize Learning, 15.* Santa Monica, CA: Author.

Recognition Ideas

28) CLASSROOM DISPLAY CASE

On the back wall of my classroom, I have set aside a large rectangular space for students to display their favorite pieces of work. In this area, known as the "Display Case," the kids each have their own spots that are roughly 15" by 15". While the idea of displaying student work on a classroom wall is certainly not new, there are two aspects of this suggestion that I believe offer a different twist on how work is traditionally shown.

First, the students are in charge of deciding what work is displayed in their individual areas, and they may update their displays at any time. This freedom and flexibility enable students to capture moments of personal triumph in "real-time" in a tangible way. For example, if a student solves a difficult math problem that took a long time to complete, she may post it in her spot right then and there. Pride, confidence, and self-esteem soar when students realize what they have accomplished and know they can place their work somewhere prominent and look at it whenever they need a boost. Families do this all the time on their refrigerators, and we can do the same in the classroom.

Second, because the kids are choosing the work that appears on the wall, the Display Case always features a wide variety of work at any given time. There is absolutely nothing wrong with bulletin boards that feature work samples from a single project, but there's something especially cool about seeing many different types of samples that the students themselves chose. Giving children the opportunity to choose their Display Case items and update them at any time builds student ownership of the classroom and reinforces the point that everyone is an important, valued part of the team.

29) STATEMENTS OF RECOGNITION

Whenever you have a few free moments at the end of a class period, ask your students to sit in a circle and point out the noteworthy efforts of their classmates. The acknowledgments can focus on academic achievements, Habits of Mind and Habits of Character, or gestures of friendship. Make sure the kids mention both whom they are recognizing and why they are recognizing that person. For instance, it's not enough for Alexis to say, "Henry." She would need to make a more specific statement, such as "I would like to recognize Henry because he has really been working hard on his math lately." Also, encourage the kids to acknowledge as many different people as possible. That way, every child experiences the pride that comes from being recognized. If you notice that certain children do not receive recognition from classmates, make it a point to acknowledge them yourself. Every child must feel valued. It's particularly nice to see how kids react when they receive a recognition from someone that they are just getting to know. In no time at all, two children can go from being strangers to friends simply because of one positive statement.

30) "WAY TO GO" NOTES

These are notes that any team member can give to any other team member for a job well done. The words "Way to Go" are printed at the top of this sheet, and there is space for the students to write their own name, the name of the person to whom they are presenting it, and the reason for giving the note. "Way to Go" notes truly bring out the best in kids, both those giving and those receiving the acknowledgment. In fact, many kids enjoy giving these notes more than they do receiving them. I'll never forget the day Sara was so excited to hand out a "Way to Go" that she built a wall of books around her desk to hide her blushing face. These papers take almost no time to fill out and to present, but the positive feelings they produce are lasting.

Kids develop very clever ways of delivering these sheets. Some will wait until after school and place a note in the recipient's desk so that they will discover it the following morning. Others will have me run interference for them as they transport the notes. For example, Chris once asked me if I could call Tiimo outside for a minute to discuss something so he could hide a "Way to Go" in Tiimo's backpack. Most kids, though, will just walk over and deliver the notes face to face. Seeing the fist bumps and smiles that accompany these exchanges is one of the highlights of my day. Sometimes we pass out the notes during our "Friday Circle" class meetings. I describe these meetings in greater detail later in the book.

Of course, you will need to establish protocols with these notes so that the kids know when it is and is not the appropriate time to write and distribute them. For example, if Miyah is listening attentively during an instructional lesson, Sunny should not get up while I'm still sharing information to acknowledge her friend's effort with a "Way to Go" note. Likewise, I would caution against using these notes during independent work time, when you want everyone to be focused on the task at hand. Generally, at the beginning of breaks or right after school are the best times.

WAY TO GO!

To:

For:

From:

31) GALLERY WALKS

Once your students have completed an art project, a math problem solving challenge, or any other type of activity in which they are demonstrating a wide variety of strategies or unique ways of thinking, consider a Gallery Walk. The Gallery Walk allows every child to see every other child's work, which, ideally, is displayed on tables that are arranged in the shape of a horseshoe or circle.

Emphasize the importance of walking slowly and quietly and paying close attention to everyone's efforts, not just those of their closest friends. To heighten students' focus, provide instructions in advance about the specific features of the work to which you want everyone to attend. A whole-class debriefing should follow a Gallery Walk, allowing kids the opportunity to describe noteworthy examples of quality work they saw, ask questions, and give compliments.

32) COMPLIMENTS

In this activity students brainstorm a list of compliments to use throughout the year. During this process we are helping the kids build the type of positive vocabulary and spirit we wish to promote in our classrooms.

Step 1: Students fold a piece of blank drawing paper into 16 squares. Independently, the kids think of all the different "compliment words" and "compliment expressions" they know and write them on their papers, one word or expression per square. The kids can use the back or fold the paper to create more squares, if necessary.

Step 2: Everyone circulates throughout the room and participates in a "Give 1, Get 1" activity where, in pairs, each child shares one idea with a partner and receives one idea from that partner before moving on to a different person. Students write these new ideas in blank squares on their papers. This exchange of ideas is a variation of an activity Ron Nash shares in *The Active Classroom*.

Step 3: The kids return to their seats for a whole-class share. As volunteers say their ideas, the teacher or student recorder lists everything on a chart for future reference while everyone else adds ideas to their papers.

Step 4: Each student circles his or her three favorite compliments, memorizes them, and commits to using them in the coming months. Follow up with these compliments as opportunities arise.

BIBLIOGRAPHY

Nash, R. (2009). *The Active Classroom*. Thousand Oaks, CA: Corwin Press.

Reifman, S. (2008). *8 Essentials for Empowered Teaching & Learning, K–8*. Thousand Oaks, CA: Corwin Press.

Reifman, S. (2013). *Rock It! Transform Classroom Learning with Movement, Songs, and Stories*. Saint Johnsbury, VT: Brigantine Media.

Movement Warmups

33) TABATA TUESDAY

Each morning my students and I participate in some type of movement warmup activity to energize our minds and bodies and prepare for a great day of learning. Two years ago, I initiated a new routine called Tabata Tuesday. It has quickly become a class favorite. A tabata is a four-minute workout consisting of eight 30-second cycles. In each cycle, participants move vigorously for 20 seconds and then rest for 10. Before we launched Tabata Tuesday, I asked each student to choose or create an exercise that they wished to include in this routine and then demonstrate that exercise using the awesome Flipgrid app that makes it so easy for us to make and share videos. I took the students' ideas and made a class list that I show on our Smart Board every Tuesday morning. Our Student Leader picks two of them for our four-minute exercise routine, and we alternate between these movements. The free Tabata app on my phone keeps track of the time, and the Beatles provide the soundtrack for one of the highlights of our week. In addition, two energetic student volunteers come to the front and serve as our Tabata leaders.

34) MACARENA THURSDAY

Perhaps the single most valuable idea I have learned in recent years, this strategy helps students improve their skip counting while performing the well-known Macarena dance. (I have found that the karaoke version on iTunes contains the best tempo for this activity.) When educator Jeff Haebig presented this idea at the physical education workshop that I attend each summer in San Luis Obispo, CA, I knew right away it was a big winner.

To prepare for this activity, create vertical strips that contain 12 multiples for every number between 3–12. Of course, depending on the grade(s) you teach, you may want to modify this range. Some sample strips are shown below. We include twelve multiples for each number because the Macarena dance has twelve parts.

3	4	6	8
6	8	12	16
9	12	18	24
12	16	24	32
15	20	30	40
18	24	36	48
21	28	42	56
24	32	48	64
27	36	54	72
30	40	60	80
33	44	66	88
36	48	72	96

Now we're ready to move. Let's begin with the 3s strip. I have my kids stand on the rug in the front of the room facing the 3s strip on the board. The music starts, and after the short introductory part of the song, we spring into action. For every part of the dance, we say a multiple of three. For example, as we turn our right palm down, we say "three." As we turn our left palm down, we say "six." As we turn our right palm up, we say "nine." The dance continues until we say the 12th multiple, 36, as we touch our left hand to our left hip. The real dance calls for participants to shimmy after the 12th multiple, but in our version we don't have time to shimmy because we have to proceed directly to the next strip.

In the beginning of the year, when the kids first learn the dance, we'll do one or two strips. Then, we'll build up to five strips. Eventually, the length of the karaoke version of the song allows us to proceed through nine strips. (We usually don't do the tens strip because the class masters it so quickly.) So, in about four minutes, the kids are seeing, saying, hearing, and moving through these multiples—and having a blast doing it. Anytime we can use all four of these modalities simultaneously, I consider it the "Educational Grand Slam" because the effect on student learning is so strong.

Macarena Thursday quickly became a class tradition. We even have parents, teachers, and administrators stopping by for occasional visits. In the time that we have been using this powerful, multi-modal strategy, student proficiency with the multiplication and division facts has improved significantly.

35) FOUR-PART MOVEMENT WARMUP

On some days my students and I participate in a four-part morning movement warmup routine that I pieced together from various sources. Executing these movements helps my students achieve what I consider to be an ideal mindset for learning: calm, relaxed, focused, and confident.

Part 1: Cross Crawls

Cross Crawls come from Paul Dennison's well-known Brain Gym program, specifically its PACE (Positive, Active, Clear, and Energetic) component. Brain Gym consists of a series of movements designed to help individuals relax, concentrate, and channel their energies in a positive direction. I like to begin our movement warmup with Cross Crawls because it is the most active of our four parts, and while it benefits everyone, I have noticed that it particularly energizes (even wakes up) those students who may enter class a bit sleepy or lethargic.

Here's how to perform Cross Crawls. Standing in place, touch the left elbow to the right knee and then the right elbow to the left knee. Continue alternating in this pattern. Cross Crawls should always be done slowly, with excellent posture and clean contact between the elbow and knee. This movement activates both hemispheres of the brain and builds nerve networks between the two hemispheres. Many kids tend to speed up while doing Cross Crawls, thinking that faster is cooler or better. Emphasize to students the importance of moving slowly as they alternate in their pattern of connecting their elbows to their opposite knees. Have your class perform this movement for about 30 seconds.

In her book *Smart Moves: Why Learning Is Not All in Your Head*, neurophysiologist and author Dr Carla Hannaford says that when children perform Cross Crawls regularly, "more nerve networks form and myelinate in the corpus callosum, thus making communication between the two hemispheres faster and more integrated for high level reasoning." Moving slowly, Hannaford says, "requires fine motor involvement and balance, consciously activating the vestibular system and frontal lobes."

Part 2: The five movement choices

For the second part of the sequence, students are given a choice of five equally valid movements, as recommended by Jeff Haebig, who introduced these movement choices to me at the same physical conference I referenced earlier. Among the many important points he made, one that stood out to me concerned students and their need to move. Rather than fight this human tendency, teachers need to accommodate it. One way I try to do this is through Part 2 of our movement warmup. This section of the warmup is a transitional step, in which children choose the type of movement they want to do, based on what they need at this time. If they need further energizing, they should opt for the first choice. If they already feel energized and ready to go, they should choose the second or fifth choice. The third and fourth choices are available to kids whose needs lie somewhere in between.

The movement choices include:

1) To energize more—<u>Big, bouncy, angular movements</u>: From a standing position, keep the upper body straight and move the head toward the left side of the waist at a 45-degree angle, come back up, then down to the right side of the waist, come back up, and repeat.

2) To calm down—<u>Slow back-and-forth rocking movements</u>: From a standing position, slowly rock the body back-and-forth in a straight line. Haebig uses the clever phrase "Rock it to calm it" to describe this movement. He also points out that when many students tip back in their chairs, this calming effect is what they are trying to

achieve. Armed with this insight, I now invite students who rock in their chairs to stand and rock to avoid the chance of falling backwards.

3) Energize and calm—<u>Combo</u>: Combine the first two in whatever manner wished in order to achieve both an energizing and calming effect.

4) <u>Stop n' go</u>: With this option students may select any of the previous choices and pause periodically as they move.

5) <u>No, thank you, I prefer to watch</u>: Some students do not need to move and should not be pressured into doing so. Standing still while others move is a perfectly legitimate choice that teachers need to honor.

Part 3: Deep breathing

After children have had the opportunity to energize themselves during the first two parts of our routine, our goal for the third and fourth parts is to help them become calm and relaxed. Deep breathing is an important part of that effort.

The basic stance for deep breathing calls for students to stand tall with one hand on their belly buttons and the other on their upper chests. I also ask students to close their eyes to help them focus on themselves, not their friends. I emphasize that the whole point of this warmup sequence is to check in with ourselves, see how we are feeling, and do what's necessary for us to have a terrific day. Many kids are understandably curious about what's going on around them and are easily distracted. So, closing the eyes is a necessary step in helping them focus their attention internally, not externally.

Quite a few variations of deep breathing exist, and kids enjoy and benefit from trying them out to determine which one(s) they may want to use on their own in the future. I describe three of these options below.

- <u>Nose vs. Mouth Breathing</u>: Try breathing in and out through only the nose, breathing through only the mouth, breathing in through the nose and out through the mouth, and breathing in through the mouth and out through the nose.
- <u>Alternate Nose Breathing</u>: Haebig suggests inhaling and exhaling while holding one nostril closed and then switching nostrils.
- <u>Rhythmical Breathing</u>: Haebig also recommends inhaling and exhaling for a certain number of counts. This option is my personal favorite because it requires a strong internal focus and helps students develop impressive control of their breathing. I suggest starting with a small number of counts and increasing the number as the kids gain proficiency.

Part 4: Hook-ups

Like Cross Crawls, Hook-ups also come from the PACE component of Paul Dennison's Brain Gym. Because Hook-ups are the final part of our movement warmup and I know we're about to head to our first academic activity (usually math), I like to add an extra dimension to this exercise. While the kids are standing in Hook-up position, I have them think about the upcoming day and focus on a specific aspect of it. Sometimes I will go through the day's schedule and ask everyone to focus on something concrete that they hope to accomplish while at school. At other times, I'll try to put the children in a good mood by asking them to think about the one or two parts of our schedule to which they are looking forward the most, even it's something like playing handball at recess. Or, I'll have them set a behavioral goal that will make a big difference in their day, such as being a better listener or remembering to ask for help when they need it. I will provide more information about our daily goals later in the book.

Here's how to perform Hook-ups. Place both arms straight out, thumbs facing down. Cross one arm over the other and interlock your fingers. Then, roll the locked hands straight down and in toward the body so they rest on the chest with elbows down. Cross one leg over the other and rest your tongue on the roof of your mouth behind the teeth. Continue breathing deeply with closed eyes. Now students are fully prepared to sit down and pay attention to the first academic lesson of the day.

Additional options

Use these movements throughout the day, either at predetermined times, such as before assessments, or as the need arises. The movements are also wonderful problem solving tools. Instead of becoming frustrated with students who have the tendency to lose their concentration and distract their classmates, I give them the option to stand outside the room for a few moments and do one or more of the movements until they have regained their focus.

I specifically recall one young boy who frequently got in trouble with previous teachers because focusing for an extended period of time was difficult for him. He would become extremely fidgety and distracting and his stress level would rise, which made it even harder for him to focus. One day, I told him that he could go outside anytime he felt himself losing focus and do one of the morning movements. He learned to get up from his chair on his own, step outside, and come back in a minute, ready to go. Once he realized that he could do this without my permission and that he was the one in total control of his behavior, his focus and confidence increased significantly.

36) WRITING WORKSHOP WARMUP

To kick off our daily Writing Workshop mini-lesson, my students and I participate in a brief movement warmup routine, created by reading specialist Debra Em Wilson, that consists of a series of hand and arm exercises. In the 30–60 seconds it takes to complete our warmup, the students are preparing both their hands and minds for a productive period of writing. As I lead my students in the hand movements, I'm encouraging them to think about what they hope to accomplish that day with whatever writing project we happen to be working on.

In addition to the physical and mental benefits our warmup provides, the routine has also taken on added value in that it has become an important class ritual that unites us as a community of writers. Some students even perform this routine on their own at other times during the day or after school when they do their homework.

Here are the various parts of our routine, followed by a brief description. The names and descriptions may differ slightly from Debra's. All parts are performed seated.

Dots: Use the thumb of one hand to push into the palm of the other hand. Each push is considered a "dot," and I encourage my students to push dots into every part of the palm. Switch sides.

Squeezes: Grab the wrist with the opposite hand and gently squeeze. Continue squeezing all the way up to the shoulder and back down to the wrist. Switch sides.

Rubbing hands: Rub the palms together to generate some heat. Then, rub the backs of the hands together to do the same thing. Next, spread apart the fingers and slide the fingers of each hand into the openings of the other hand. Turn the hands and slide the backs of each hand together into the openings of the other hand.

Claps and pats: Clap the hands together and then keep clapping as you slide the hands to the opposite wrists and up the opposite arm. Pat the skin from the wrists all the way up to the shoulders and back down.

Gloves: As if you and your students are putting on imaginary writing gloves, use the thumb and index finger of one hand to touch the skin of each finger on the opposite hand from fingertip to wrist. Switch sides.

Grab and resist: Interlace the fingers of each hand as you push your two palms together. Then try to pull your hands away from each other, but don't let go. Resisting in this manner should cause you to feel your shoulders and upper back working.

Listening position: With the hands still attached from the previous movement, I ask everyone to put their hands under their chin, place their elbows on their knees, and look up at the board as I begin my instruction. Transitioning to the final movement in this manner greatly increases the likelihood that my students will demonstrate strong eye contact as I start the lesson.

37) READING WORKSHOP WARMUP

This warmup sequence was inspired by legendary physical education instructor Chip Candy. I use it prior to my daily Reading Workshop mini-lesson, but you can use it to kick off any type of lesson. It works well to have students perform this routine twice in a row, the first time while standing and the second time as they transition to a seated position.

Sequence: Students alternate hands and touch their opposite ears, shoulders, hips, knees, and feet. In doing so, every move they make crosses the midline as they proceed from their heads to their feet. Specifically, the kids touch their right hands to their left ears, left hands to their right ears, right hands to left shoulders, left hands to right shoulders, right hands to left hips, left hands to right hips, right hands to left knees, left hands to right knees, right hands to left feet, and left hands to right feet. They say the name of each body part as they touch it.

After the final move, the students say, "PACE," which is an acronym to promote attentive listening (P = Posture, A = Attention, C = Careful listening, E = Eye contact). As the kids say "PACE," they put their hands under their chins and elbows on their knees and look up at the board. If you and your students proceed through this sequence twice, here is what the warmup routine sounds like from beginning to end: "Ear, ear, shoulder, shoulder, hip, hip, knee, knee, foot, foot, ear, ear, shoulder, shoulder, hip, hip, knee, knee, foot, foot, PACE!"

And now everyone's ready to get to work.

BIBLIOGRAPHY

Dennison, P. and Dennison, G. (2010). *Brain Gym® Teacher's Edition*. Ventura, CA: Hearts at Play, Inc.

Hannaford, C. (1995). *Smart Moves: Why Learning Is Not All in Your Head*. Arlington, VA: Great Ocean Publishers.

Heiniger-White, M. and Wilson, D. (2010). *S'cool Moves for Learning*. Shasta, CA: Integrated Learner Press.

Reifman, S. (2013). *Rock It! Transform Classroom Learning with Movement, Songs, and Stories*. Saint Johnsbury, VT: Brigantine Media.

Parent Involvement Ideas

38) BE PROACTIVE IN YOUR COMMUNICATIONS WITH PARENTS

Being proactive has two major benefits. First, it gives you the opportunity to package your ideas and articulate them in the best possible light. Acting first, you shape the conversation, saying your ideas in the way you want to say them, not in the way someone else has already characterized them before ever having the chance to hear from you. Being proactive increases your credibility, strengthens your voice, and reaffirms your position of leadership.

Second, being proactive is the best approach to problem prevention. Consider the following example. Imagine that a brand new shipment of expensive, state-of-the-art math manipulatives has just arrived at school. Because the school could afford only one set, the staff decided that each class would get the manipulatives for three weeks. When our turn comes, I lengthen the daily math period from 45 minutes to 90 minutes so we can try all the hands-on activities shown in the accompanying teacher guidebook. To compensate for the extra time that we spend on math, I don't give any math homework for the next three weeks.

Immediately, parents become concerned. "Where's my child's math homework?" they ask. "Why did you stop assigning math homework?" they wonder. "Don't you know that my child will fall behind without math practice every night?" they insist.

Now, I have to react. The parents have already made up their minds. Based on the information they have received from their kids, they have concluded that I have stopped assigning math homework, and they don't understand why. I have dug myself a hole, out of which I must climb.

All this trouble could have been avoided had I been proactive. Before the first day of our three-week manipulative exploration, I should have sent home a newsletter explaining the situation. Then, the parents would have known in advance of the unique, short-term opportunity that we had to use these manipulatives and understood the value of these types of experiences. I could have told them that to take full advantage of this opportunity, I would be lengthening our daily math period, and that because of the extra time the kids spent on math in class, I would be decreasing the time they spend on math at home. I could have emphasized that this hiatus from math homework would last only three weeks and that the kids would not be at all disadvantaged because they were gaining valuable practice in class. Informing parents beforehand would have enabled me to accentuate the positive.

Experience has taught me that teachers' greatest difficulties with parents often arise from a lack of proactivity. When parents are not informed in advance about rules, units, grading policies, and the like, they have every reason to come back after the fact and say, "I didn't know." Once that happens, teachers are forced into a reactive, often defensive, position. The trouble is, no matter how effectively we later explain ourselves, the damage has already been done. Furthermore, by the time we have responded to one problem situation, the next crisis has occurred and needs to be addressed. A pattern soon begins. We find ourselves spending a tremendous amount of time putting out fires instead of using it to communicate proactively.

39) PARENT CONFERENCE PREVIEW VIDEO

A few years ago, I created a short "Parent Conference Preview Video" to provide background information about the various items I discuss at my school's November parent meetings. By explaining our class rubrics, scoring systems, and general practices in advance, I can reduce the time I spend at the conferences on general information and increase the time I spend on information that specifically relates to each child's progress. I encourage the parents to watch the video with their children since the kids attend the conference with their parents. I reuse the same video each year. Should any agenda item change from one year to the next, I simply note it in the same email that includes the link to the video. I have noticed a significant difference in the quality of our conferences since I started using the video, and I encourage you to give it a try. You can see the one I created on YouTube.[1]

40) TEACH KIDS TO COMPLETE HOMEWORK INDEPENDENTLY

When assisting students with their math activities and other academic work, it is often difficult for teachers to know how much help to provide. The same is true for parents supervising their children's homework. If we don't offer enough assistance, students' struggles are likely to continue, and kids may become frustrated and discouraged. They may even shut down. On the other hand, if we provide too much assistance, students may complete their work successfully, but, in the process, we may deny them opportunities to think for themselves and develop as independent thinkers and problem solvers.

To strike a balance, it helps to think about a comparable situation that happens in gyms all the time with weightlifters. Consider the bench press exercise in which people lie on their backs on a flat bench and attempt to push a barbell from their chests into the air for a certain number of repetitions.

Imagine my friend is trying to bench press 20 pounds 10 times. Because the weight is so light, he can easily complete the set on his own. When the amount of weight increases, however, he needs me to spot for him so that the barbell doesn't remain on his chest when he reaches the point of muscle failure.

Assume that when trying to bench press 185 pounds, my friend's goal is to complete 8 repetitions. He finishes the first 6 reps on his own, yet struggles halfway through his seventh. I am standing behind him the entire time with my hands underneath the bar, ready to assist. In this situation I have a choice to make, and I basically have three options. First, I can do nothing, but if I choose this approach, the barbell will come down on his chest, an injury is likely to occur, and our friendship may end.

On the other hand, I can take over and finish the rep for him. If I simply grab the bar at the first sign of struggle and return it to the weight rack on my own, I ensure his safety, but I have done nothing to help him improve his strength. As a result, the next time he bench presses, there is no reason to expect that he will be able to lift any more weight than he did this time.

The best approach in this situation is for me to put my hands under the barbell and do as little work as possible to help him keep the bar moving. If he's able to do most of the work himself, my effort will be very gentle. If his struggle increases, I will assume more of the workload. I will continue to adjust the amount of assistance I provide based on the amount of work he is able to do for himself.

If he needs only a small amount of assistance on the seventh rep, he may choose to try for an eighth, and on that rep I will probably have to increase the amount of support I provide. The strength gains that this set produces occur mostly in these final two reps, not the first six that he could do independently. My performance as a spotter helps him go beyond what he could do independently to move to that next level of strength. The next time he bench presses, he will probably be able to do more of the work on his own because of the assistance I provided this time around.

These moments of struggle are crucial growth opportunities, and by carefully providing just enough guidance to help keep the bar moving, I am empowering my friend to move beyond his current capacity to a larger future capacity.

In the classroom, moments of struggle need to be savored as valuable growth opportunities. As teachers, if we are able to provide just enough assistance to keep students moving forward, we increase their capacity for the future. Sometimes that little assistance involves asking the right question, suggesting an appropriate strategy, offering encouragement, or reminding them to try an approach that they may have used successfully in the past. It never means abandoning them, and it never means telling them what to do.

We simply want to keep the bar moving.

Share this "bench press analogy" with parents at "Back to School Night" and in your ongoing home–school communications.

41) "WHILE YOU WERE ABSENT" SHEETS

An important part of holding students accountable for their learning involves making sure they complete the projects and activities that occurred while they were absent. Whenever my students miss a day of school, I write down all the work they need to make up on a "While You Were Absent" sheet. I place this sheet on their desks, along with the books, papers, and other materials they will need in order to complete everything described on the sheet. You can find a copy of this sheet below and on Routledge.com.

Usually, I fill out these sheets each morning during our silent reading period. At this time I also meet, one-on-one, with the students who are returning from an absence so I can discuss with them everything I wrote on their sheet. Sometimes I will have the students take their make-up work home, while other times I will have them work on the activities in class, as time permits. My decision depends on the complexity of the task, whether my students will need access to certain materials, the number of days the students missed, and whether participation in a task later that day depends on completion of a task they missed.

I encourage parents to come to the classroom at the end of each day their child misses (or send a sibling or trusted friend) to collect the work so that everything can be made up expeditiously, though I fully understand this is not always possible. Since I started using these sheets many years ago, I have been better able to keep track of my students' work and ensure they remain caught up with regard to our state content standards.

Name _____ Date _____

While You Were Absent

_____

_____

_____

_____

_____

_____

_____

Name _____ Date _____

While You Were Absent

_____

_____

_____

_____

_____

_____

_____

42) READY-MADE PARENT EMAILS

At designated times during every school year, I send important information to parents via email. These messages pertain to such events as Back to School Night, parent conferences, and writing celebrations and such topics as project deadlines, upcoming assessments, and report cards. Some of these correspondences are quite long and detailed. Rather than begin from scratch each year, I realized that I could paste these messages into a word processing file and use them as my starting point in future years. Using these "ready-made" parent emails saves me a tremendous amount of time and guarantees that I will remember to include all the major points I want to mention.

43) BEGIN WITH A BANG

Prior to my second year of teaching, I came across an idea I just had to try. First, I obtained a class list with my first graders' names and phone numbers. With permission from my administrator, I went home and called every family, introducing myself to the parents and telling them that I was tentatively scheduled to be their child's teacher that year. I used the word *tentatively* to cover myself and the school in case any last-minute enrollment changes were made. Since I knew I'd be setting up the classroom during the week before school started, I invited each family to stop by to meet me in person. About 10 of my 32 students accepted this offer. With these 10, I was able to learn their names, talk with them briefly, and get a sense of who they were. I greatly enjoyed and appreciated this one-on-one time.

I then found the previous year's Kindergarten class pictures in the yearbook. By matching the names on my list to the faces in the yearbook, I learned the names of the rest of my returning students. In addition, I was expecting only two new students, one boy and one girl. So, I quickly learned their names. The night before school started, I made a simple name tag for each child and arranged the tags on a table by the front door of the classroom.

The next morning, I was ready. I stood at the door eager to welcome my new students. While I was praying that none of them had gotten haircuts over the summer, they began to arrive. I greeted each one by name, handed them a name tag, and invited them to sit down on the rug. Standing outside on the yard, a number of parents watched the whole thing, wondering how I could possibly know the names of people I had never met. I felt fantastic. Before the school year was barely three minutes old, I had created a very favorable first impression with my students and their parents. This proactive gesture had set the tone I wanted.

Begin the year with some sort of powerful, dramatic initiative. If you are unable to obtain a class list before the start of the year, do something the first day. Write a short, personalized note to each student, call each parent after school to express how much you are looking forward to the year ahead, or send a postcard through the mail. Just do something. The more novel, the better. A thoughtful gesture on your part will be remembered.

If you're reading this book well after the start of the school year, you can still use one of the aforementioned ideas or come up with something of your own. Our relationships with students and their parents can always be strengthened.

NOTE

1   https://www.youtube.com/watch?v=xu8KAGXDz6g&t=1s

BIBLIOGRAPHY

Reifman, S. (2008). *8 Essentials for Empowered Teaching & Learning, K–8*. Thousand Oaks, CA: Corwin Press.

PART 2

Improve Academic Instruction

Language Arts Ideas

44) READING NOTEBOOKS WITH INSERTS

Many teachers ask their students to keep a weekly log of the independent reading they do at home and return the sheets on Fridays. This routine holds children accountable and provides valuable information about everyone's nightly productivity (i.e., minutes spent and pages read). Two challenges exist with this practice. First, students sometimes lose these individual sheets. Second, looking through 20–30 logs at once and finding the time to offer immediate, one-on-one feedback can be difficult.

Instead of having kids fill out weekly log sheets, I suggest giving each child a reading notebook for all of their recordings. Specifically, students should use a new page for each book they choose and, for each session, write down the date, starting time, ending time, number of minutes read, starting page, ending page, and number of pages read. Inside the front cover of the notebook, I paste the insert shown below so the kids can see where to write the title, author, and book level and how to set up all the columns.

Bridge to Terabithia By Katherine Paterson						T
Date	ST	ET	#M	SP	EP	#P
8/26	10:00	10:40	40	1	29	29
8/26	6:15	6:55	40	29	60	31
8/27	10:05	10:45	40	61	92	32
8/27	5:45	6:25	40	92	121	29
8/28	10:02	10:42	40	121	153	32
8/28	5:01	5:41	40	153	182	29
8/29	10:07	10:47	40	182	(208)	36

This method presents two advantages. First, because students take home both their books and reading notebooks in a large Ziploc bag each day, it is unlikely that anything will be lost. In fact, over the years I can recall very few times when a child lost their reading notebook. The other advantage is that since children have their notebooks with them every day, we can ask each child to check in with us briefly each time they finish a book. Because children finish books at different rates, our check-ins will naturally be staggered throughout the week, making it easier for us to follow up. In addition, we can maintain a page in our planner or grading book and write the date every time a child finishes a book. That way, if it seems as if some children haven't completed a book in a while, our records will tell us that, and we can follow up as needed.

45) THREE DIMENSIONAL CHARACTER BONE STRUCTURE

In fiction writing, once children have chosen their story ideas, they can begin the important work of bringing their characters to life so readers find them interesting and care about what happens to them. During my years as a teacher, I have learned that many kids think character description is the part of the story in which we just say what the people look like. Usually, these descriptions focus on only hair color and eye color.

That's a nice start, but bringing our characters to life involves much more than simple physical descriptions. Rather, our goal with this aspect of writing involves bringing to life the whole person and focuses on what makes each character unique and memorable. Yes, we want to know what the characters look like, but we also want to know how they act, how they handle different situations, and what makes them tick.

To help kids meet this challenge, I made a special tool called the Three-Dimensional Bone Structure. It is called "three-dimensional" because it has three parts or "bones." Taken together, these parts enable students to develop well-rounded characters. Here are the three parts of the Bone Structure:

1. The "Psychological" bone is the part of the sheet on which we describe the character's personality or "mind features."
2. The "Sociological" bone is the part of the sheet on which we describe the character's family background or "family features."
3. The "Physiological" bone is the part of the sheet on which we describe what the character looks like or "physical features."

Young writers can fill out the Bone Structure for their main character, as well as secondary characters, if you wish. Kids don't need to write something for every part of the sheet, but they should have at least a few things on each bone. If your students do complete each part, they may begin to think that their character actually exists. If they don't, their characters may not seem real, and readers may not care about them as much.

A small representation of the bone structure is shown below, and you can find a full-page version for free on my TeachersPayTeachers page.[1]

Name _____

Date _____

Three-Dimensional Character Bone Structure

Psychological (mind features)	Sociological (family features)
• Hopes and ambitions: • Fears/frustrations: • Hobbies: • Strengths: • Weaknesses: • Temperament (e.g., easygoing, calm fiery, optimistic, pessimistic): • Unique personality traits (What makes this person tick?):	• Job/responsibilities: • Race/ethnicity: • Religion: • Income level: • Home life (e.g., parents, siblings): • Pets:

Physiological (body features)

- Name:

- Gender:

- Age:

- Hair color:

- Eye color:

- Appearance (e.g., neat, messy, tall, short, skinny):

- Typical clothing:

- Distinguishing features (e.g., freckles, eyeglasses, birthmarks, braces):

46) FOUR-COLOR EDITING

Editing is typically one of the most difficult stages of the writing process for students because it requires so much attention to detail. For many children the task can be overwhelming simply because they are asked to look for so many different types of mistakes at the same time, such as those related to capitalization, punctuation, paragraphing, dialogue, and spelling.

A while ago I came up with a new approach that breaks down the complex task of editing into smaller, more manageable steps. Since that time my students have become more willing, more enthusiastic, more successful editors of their own writing. I call my approach "Four-Color Editing."

Each student needs a four-color ballpoint pen and an Editing Checklist. You can find a sample Editing Checklist on the following page and on Routledge.com. The checklist comes from a TeachersPayTeachers item I created that contains different versions that you may want to use in your classroom. You can find it on that website.[2]

Each checklist is divided into four different sections, with every section corresponding to a specific color of the pen. For example, in the first section the students use the black pen as they read through their project searching for mistakes involving indenting and the punctuation of dialogue.

In the second section students use red as they read through their work again and search for run-on sentences and other mistakes involving commas and end punctuation. Blue is the color students use in the third section as they read their work a third time and search for mistakes of capitalization. I break down sections two and three even further by including specific occasions when commas and capitals are necessary. I change these sections throughout the year to reflect the rules we are learning at the time.

Finally, students use green to focus on spelling. In this step I ask the students to point to each word and circle the ones they aren't 100% sure about. Then the kids get dictionaries to look up these words.

The kids check off each part of each section as they proceed through the Editing Checklist.

Four-Color Editing Checklist

<u>Directions:</u> Check off each line as you use your four-color pen to complete the Editing Checklist.

Black is the color for **indented paragraphs.**
<u>What to do</u>: Check to see if all your paragraphs are indented.
_____ I checked to see if all my paragraphs are indented.
_____ I put a paragraph symbol (¶) next to all paragraphs where I forgot to indent in my draft so that I remember to indent when I publish.

Red is the color for **run-on sentences** and **other punctuation.**
<u>What to do</u>: Read your work aloud to yourself. Correct any run-on sentences you find. Also, check that you have commas, question marks, and exclamation points in the right places.
_____ I found and corrected all my run-on sentences.
_____ I have commas, question marks, and exclamation points in the right places.

Blue is the color for **capitals.**
<u>What to do</u>: Read your work aloud to yourself a second time. Check to see that you have capitals:
_____ at the beginning of every sentence.
_____ for all names of people, places, and things.
_____ for the word *I.*
_____ for days of the week and months of the year.
_____ for all titles and holidays.

Green is the color for **spelling.**
<u>What to do</u>: Read your work aloud a third time. Point to each word carefully. Circle any word you are not 100% sure about. Then check these words in the dictionary.
_____ I pointed to each word and circled all the words I wasn't 100% sure about.
_____ I used a dictionary to correct all misspelled words.

Practice

my favorite type of salad is a Caesar salad. I order it whenever i go to an Italian restaurant the dressing is the best part. crunchy croutons ar allso a terrific part off the salad. The iceberg lettuce is allso very crunchy the crunch makes a cool sound. Sometimes the server actuly comes to your table and creeaytes the salad while you watch. i can't wate to order a caesar salad the next time i go out to eat

47) HELP STUDENTS LEARN TO SPEAK AND WRITE IN COMPLETE SENTENCES

Speaking and writing in complete sentences tends to be challenging for many children. I find it helpful to begin my instruction in this area by focusing on how students respond to written questions. Two strategies have proven to be especially effective. For example, imagine you ask a child, "What was your favorite part of the book?" The first strategy I recommend is to take the words from the question and use them to begin the answer. That usually will lead children to form a complete sentence. A child using this strategy might respond by saying, "My favorite part of the book was the ending."

A second strategy is to start with the word *I*. When starting with *I*, inevitably the child will follow with a verb and then continue by finishing their thought. So, returning to the book question, a child employing this strategy might respond by saying "I" and then use a verb such as *liked* or *enjoyed* and then say "the ending."

NOTES

1 https://www.teacherspayteachers.com/Product/Developing-Well-Rounded-Characters-in-Reading-and-Writing-Workshop-388374
2 https://www.teacherspayteachers.com/Product/Editing-Checklists-to-Use-with-the-4-Color-Pen-Approach-412885

Learn English Language Arts Concepts through Movement

48) THE SYNONYM–ANTONYM SIDESTEP

This activity was inspired by Elly Goldman and Denise Schiavone. Before you begin this activity with your class, prepare a set of approximately 20 index cards with a word pair written on each—either synonyms or antonyms of each other. Possible synonym pairs could include *great–excellent* and *happy–cheerful*; possible antonym pairs could include *up–down* and *hot–cold*. Since the focus of this activity is on understanding the concept of synonyms and antonyms, not vocabulary, it's fine to use word pairs that may be easy for your students. Below you will find the full set of word pairs that I use.

The students stand in two lines, one on each side of the room, and face the center. The middle of the room needs to remain open because the kids will be moving through this area. Place the stack of index cards face down on the floor near the front wall. The first person in each line walks to the pile and, together, the two kids select the top card. The rest of the students slide up one place in line every time a new pair of students comes to the front to get a card.

The two kids in the front of the room then stand shoulder to shoulder, read the word pair aloud, and decide if the words on their card are synonyms or antonyms. If the words are synonyms, the partners face each other, grab hands, sidestep through the middle of the room, and go to the end of their respective lines. If the words are antonyms, the kids go back-to-back (facing opposite directions), grab hands, sidestep through the center, and go back to the end of their lines. As the game progresses, the idea is that the kids will associate the term *synonym* with the word *same* (because the two sidesteppers are facing the same direction) and the term *antonym* with the word *opposite* (because they're facing the opposite direction). Repeat this idea throughout the game. To keep the children who are waiting in line engaged in the activity and to provide valuable reinforcement of these concepts, have everyone clap and chant either "syn-o-nym" or "ant-o-nym" each time a new pair of students sidesteps through the middle of the room.

Suggested word pairs:	
Synonym pairs	Antonym pairs
happy–cheerful	up–down
rich–wealthy	hot–cold
smart–intelligent	optimistic–pessimistic
gigantic–large	clean–dirty
kind–nice	straight–crooked
tasty–delicious	sharp–dull
fantastic–wonderful	in–out
cruel–unkind	generous–selfish
hot–boiling	fast–slow
tiny–small	over–under

49) THE JUMPING GAME

The Jumping Game is another synonym–antonym activity. Prepare a list of words, typically two to four per ten-minute session, for which your students can think of synonyms and antonyms.

Have the kids form pairs and then face their partners. They should stand a few feet away from their partners, with adequate space between each pair. Then announce the first "go" word. The kids jump up and down on two feet twice, and then stick out one leg. It's like playing rock-paper-scissors with feet. If the partners show opposite legs (their legs make a diagonal line when their feet meet toe-to-toe), they think of as many antonyms as possible for the "go" word and say them quietly to each other. If they show legs from the same side of their bodies (their legs make a straight line when their feet meet toe-to-toe), they brainstorm synonyms. To keep the kids jumping at the same speed as their partners, call out, "Jump once, jump twice, show."

Let's assume the first "go" word is *mean*. The kids jump once, jump twice, and show their feet. The pairs who show "same-side" legs brainstorm synonyms, such as *cruel*, *rotten*, and *unkind*. The pairs who show "opposite" legs brainstorm antonyms, such as *friendly*, *kind*, and *nice*. Give the groups about 30 seconds to think of their synonyms and antonyms before bringing everyone together for a quick whole-class share. Check for accuracy, reinforce the meaning of the two terms, and compliment students who demonstrate excellent word choice.

50) READING AROUND THE ROOM

Comprehension often suffers when children read too quickly or fail to follow punctuation signals. To address these issues, use this activity adapted from Patricia Wolfe's book *Brain Matters: Translating Research into Classroom Practice* as cited in Marcia Tate's book *Worksheets Don't Grow Dendrites*. Students stand in a large circle with a common text in their hands. On the "go" signal, everyone reads aloud, in unison, from a predetermined starting point. While reading, everyone slowly walks forward. At every comma, students stop walking and pause in their reading for one second before resuming their walking and reading. At every period, exclamation point, or question mark, the kids stop and pause in their reading for two seconds before resuming their walking and reading. You may need to create additional movements or gestures for hyphens, quotation marks, and other types of punctuation you and your students may encounter. Reading and moving together provides a strong physical and vocal structure that helps children who may struggle to follow these rules. This activity helps everyone read with better fluency, volume, and expression. Even three minutes per day for a couple of weeks makes a huge difference in student reading proficiency.

51) THE SLOUCH GAME

The Slouch Game helps students distinguish between proper nouns (which begin with capital letters because they name specific people, places, and things) and common nouns (which do not require capitals). The game begins with everyone seated in chairs. Call out a noun. If it is a proper noun, the kids sit up tall in their chairs to mimic a capital letter. If it is a common noun, the kids slouch because the noun starts with a lower-case letter. Kids love the novelty of this activity because teachers and parents are constantly telling them to sit up straight, but now they are required to slouch as part of the game.

In the beginning of the activity, alternate between common nouns and their corresponding proper nouns in order to establish an easy-to-follow pattern, build student confidence, and give the kids a nice mini-workout. For example, you could start with the following words: city (slouch), Los Angeles (sit tall), school (slouch), Roosevelt School (sit tall), team (slouch), Dodgers (sit tall). Once you have established a pattern, break it so the students must listen and think more carefully. Call out nouns at random, with no concern as to whether they are common or proper. You can quickly assess which students may need more follow up with these concepts.

Children who struggle with differentiating these types of nouns are able to correct their mistakes easily, since they can look around and observe what the other students are doing. The Slouch Game also works when students are learning other capitalization rules. Caution everyone to be careful with their lower backs as they play the game.

52) THE CONTRACTION BLUES

The Contraction Blues is a whole-class letter game that helps students learn about contractions. The game helps children understand that when two words are contracted, one or more letters are taken away, and the resulting word is shorter than the two original words. Many kids struggle with contractions because they either put the apostrophe in the wrong place or omit it entirely. As a preface to this game, introduce the word *contract* and emphasize that when something contracts, it gets smaller or shorter. To demonstrate this concept, find a student wearing short sleeves, call that child to the front of the room, and have them extend their arm straight out. With your fingers, measure the length of the student's arm from the shoulder to the elbow. Ask the student to flex the bicep. Most kids will look to see the height of the muscle, but encourage everyone to focus on how the contraction of the bicep makes the length of the muscle shorter. Emphasize that when something contracts, it gets shorter.

To play the Contraction Blues, you need individual letter cards. You can make these using large index cards. Give each student a letter card. (If you have more than 26 students, you can make extra *l*'s, *n*'s, and vowels in the event these letters are needed to spell certain words.) Start by calling out the words *is* and *not*. The students with those letters come to the front of the room, hold their cards in front of them for the class to see, and stand shoulder to shoulder to spell out the words while leaving a space between them. Choose a volunteer, known as the Contractor, who springs into action. The Contractor: 1) determines which unlucky cardholder needs to sit back down because they are in possession of the letter *o*, which is dropped when *is* and *not* contract to form *isn't*; and 2) escorts that now unnecessary person off the stage. Naturally, kids love being the Contractor. They love tapping someone on the shoulder and politely informing the person that their services are, for the time being, no longer required.

The holder of the *o* then sadly returns to their spot. Keep tissues nearby to help the exiting student deal with the emotional pain of being contracted and cope with, you guessed it, "the Contraction Blues." Let the kids ham it up and have fun playing up the drama.

Once that unpleasantness is over, the Contractor steps in between the *n* and the *t* and forms an apostrophe with their hand while the holders of the *i* and the *s* move closer to the others to eliminate the space that separates the two words. This physical shortening is crucial. Now the class has a chance to see the contracted word *isn't* with the apostrophe in the right place and with the resulting contraction physically shorter than the two words that made it. Repeat this point about the shortening of the word so the students understand the meaning of the word contraction. Proceed through a few additional examples so more children can have a turn coming up to the front of the room and so the kids can see this shortening principle reinforced. Start with simple examples such as *I'm* and *wasn't* and then proceed to more complicated contractions, such as *she'll* and *won't*. To prevent the students holding letters such as *x* or *q* from being left out, ask them to serve as Contractors or give them the aforementioned extra letters.

53) PREFIX–SUFFIX CARDS

This activity is an example of Index Card Arranging, a type of strategy that helps kids understand a wide variety of language arts concepts. The basic idea calls for students to arrange individual index cards into sequences. Index Card Arranging is appropriate for sequencing events of a story, placing words in alphabetical order, arranging words in a sentence with proper syntax, dividing the syllables in a word, assembling smaller words into compound words, working with prefix-base word-suffix combinations, reuniting words from the same word families, matching rhyming words, and categorizing items.

My favorite application of this strategy works well for teaching prefix-base word-suffix combinations. Create and laminate a set of red cards with prefixes on the front and their meanings on the back, yellow cards with base words, and blue cards with suffixes on the front and their meanings on the back. (You can find the set I created on TeachersPayTeachers.[1]) Give each student one or more cards and call out a word, such as *careful*. The child with the *care* card joins the one with the *ful* suffix card at the front of the room to form the word *careful*. Seeing the two parts of the word in different colors come together provides children with a visual and kinesthetic way to understand prefixes and suffixes.

It's fun to end each session of this activity with the "Randomizer." Call three kids at random—one who's holding a prefix, one with a base word, and one with a suffix—to bring their cards to the front of the room. They put their cards together to form (usually) a nonsense word. The kids LOVE seeing what these random word parts create, and there is something about the silliness of the idea that legitimately reinforces both the meaning of the specific parts and the general concept of smaller parts coming together to make a larger word.

54) ACTIVE DLR (DAILY LANGUAGE REVIEW)

A terrific way to incorporate more "active learning" into our classrooms is to employ a strategy inspired by well-known presenter Jean Moize. My students and I use it frequently during our 10–15 minute "word work" sessions that conclude our Reading Workshop period a few days a week. In the past the kids would sit on the rug during word work and gain practice with a variety of spelling, capitalization, punctuation, and grammar concepts by correcting sentences on a sheet that I would provide. We would then come together as a group to go over the correct answers.

Now, instead of working alone, every child has a partner, and the pairs begin each sentence in a standing position. Before the kids sit down to make the corrections together, they "move through" the sentence by acting out specific movements that correspond to the types of changes they need to make. For example, as they read the sentence aloud, the kids spin in a circle every time they encounter a misspelled word. When we correct misspellings on the paper, we circle the word and write the correct version above the circle. So, the spinning corresponds to the circling they do on the paper. Below you will find other examples of movements we do for different types of corrections. You and your students can also create your own.

Once the pairs have had a couple minutes to move through the sentences and make the corrections on their papers, we go over the answers together as a class. Finally, we stand once again and move through the sentence as a group. That way, we have one more opportunity to reinforce the correct answers, and since the kids are already standing, they're ready to proceed directly to the next sentence. Incorporating movement has added tremendous energy and engagement to our word work, and the kids are paying greater attention to detail than they did under our more sedentary approach. In addition, working with partners allows the kids to help one another more easily and provides an important sense of belonging. In short, the kids are learning more, bonding more, and displaying greater enthusiasm with this active approach.

- To show that we need to indent, we do a skier's jump from left to right.
- To change a lower-case letter to a capital, we duck down to the ground and then rise up and extend our arms (as if doing the wave).
- To change a capital letter to lower case, we start with our arms extended above our heads and duck down to the ground.
- To insert a comma, we hop on one foot.
- To insert a period, we jump on two feet.
- To insert a question mark, we jump on two feet with our palms facing up (as if asking a question).
- To insert an exclamation point, we jump on two feet with great energy to show strong emotion.

NOTE

1 https://www.teacherspayteachers.com/Product/Prefix-Base-Word-and-Suffix-Cards-406957

BIBLIOGRAPHY

Moize, Jean. (2000). *Thinking on Your Feet: 100+ Activities That Make Learning a Moving Experience.* Murphy, TX: Action Based Learning.

Reifman, S. (2013). *Rock It! Transform Classroom Learning with Movement, Songs, and Stories.* Saint Johnsbury, VT: Brigantine Media.

Tate, M. (2010). *Worksheets Don't Grow Dendrites.* Thousand Oaks, CA: Corwin Press.

Wolfe, P. (2001). *Brain Matters: Translating Research into Classroom Practice.* Alexandria, VA: Association for Supervision and Curriculum Development.

Math Ideas

55) MATH PROBLEM SOLVING MENUS

Whenever my students finish their daily math activity early, they proceed directly to their Math Problem Solving Menus and work on them until the end of the period. Since I discovered this idea several years ago, it has been one of the most effective parts of our overall math curriculum. Each menu is a sheet with four open-ended story problems that call on students to employ a wide variety of strategies. I found some of these menu problems in various resources. Others I adapted or created from scratch.

In my upper grade classroom, there are nine menus in the set, and the students strive to complete as many of the nine as possible before the end of the year. The menus begin with straightforward, multi-step problems involving addition and subtraction. From there, the menus increase in difficulty and complexity. Many of the problems connect to and extend concepts we are learning in class, while others feature concepts and require strategies that go beyond our state's content standards.

Using Math Problem Solving Menus helps me accomplish four primary objectives. First, the menus keep my students productively engaged and occupied. Many times, kids lose focus at the end of a math period because they know they have completed the important work and think that anything they do after that is less important. That doesn't happen with the menus.

Second, many of the menu problems offer valuable reinforcement, extra practice, and meaningful review of important content that we learned earlier in the year. Plus, because each menu problem features an engaging story or situation, the kids are applying their skills and using them in context.

Third, the menus are differentiated. Because high-achieving math students tend to finish daily math work faster than their classmates, they will spend more time working on their menus and progress to the more difficult ones sooner. Kids who experience difficulty with core concepts usually spend less time on their menus, and that is OK because these students need more time to master the basics. So, in a typical math period, everyone is working at an appropriate level of challenge for the entire time. (Note: students who aren't spending much class time on their menus are welcome to take them home so that they don't lose out on this valuable experience, and many kids have done so over the years.)

Finally, because each menu is part of the larger set of nine, there is a year-long cohesiveness to this activity. I have heard many educators say that school should be more like a video game. In video games, kids are always engaged because they are constantly trying to move to a higher level. The step-by-step nature of video games ensures that kids are optimally challenged and never bored. Progressing through the nine menus offers children this same experience in school. In addition, it promotes goal setting and an achievement orientation. Trying to complete all nine menus before the end of the year becomes a meaningful, shared classroom goal.

My students use a template I created when completing the math problem solving challenges. By proceeding through the steps of this process carefully, the kids are gaining valuable practice with a wide variety of important skills.

I have included a copy of this template, along with a sample menu. A printable version can be found at Routledge.com. On TeachersPayTeachers, you will find my "Math Problem Solving Menus" item that contains the full set of menus, a scoring rubric, suggested strategies, a description of the steps students need to follow on the template, an answer key, and other important information explaining how to incorporate the menus into your teaching.[1]

Name _____ Date _____

Problem Solving Organizer for

The _____ Problem

Question: _____

_____?

Important Facts: (It may be easier to use key words and phrases than complete
sentences.)

1) _____

2) _____

3) _____

4) _____

Conditions: (Conditions are special rules. Just write "N/A" if there aren't any conditions.)

1) _____

2) _____

3) _____

Choose a Strategy: (Tell which strategy you are using and show work in the space below.)
Name of my strategy: _____

Solution (labeled):

Is your solution reasonable? (Be sure to check your work carefully.)   Yes   No

Name _____

Problem Solving Menu #1

The Train Problem

When Brittany's train left the station, 75 seats were filled. At the next stop 34 people got on the train. 35 more people got on the train at the next stop. 69 people got off the train at the next stop. 75 more people got on the train at the next stop. How many people are currently on the train?

The Parking Lot Problem

30 cars were parked in the Santa Monica Beach parking lot. An hour later 50 more cars came into the lot and parked. Soon after, 36 more cars came into the lot and parked. At the end of the day, 50 cars left the parking lot. How many cars are in the parking lot now?

The Auditorium Problem

The 20 kids in Room 34 went to the auditorium for an assembly. 100 kids were already there when Room 34 arrived. After that, Mrs. Snow's and Mrs. Whitley's 52 kids came into the auditorium. Then, 23 more kids entered the auditorium. Before the show started, 30 students had to leave the auditorium. How many kids are currently in the auditorium?

The Paper Problem

Mr. Sanchez bought 35 pieces of paper for a special writing activity. When it was time for the special activity, he gave each student 1 piece of paper. There were only 16 kids at school that day. After lunch, 3 teachers came, and they each borrowed 3 pieces of that paper. How many pieces of paper did Mr. Sanchez have left?

56) COMPENSATION

One of the most challenging tasks for young math students involves subtraction with zeroes. For example, when subtracting 1,234 from 3,000, children who use the standard algorithm need to regroup several times to get their answer. A fantastic alternative to this algorithm is a strategy known as compensation. The first step of this approach is simply to subtract one from the 3,000 to turn it into 2,999. Now, no regrouping is needed to carry out the subtraction and arrive at 1,765. At the end, students add back the one to get the correct answer of 1,766. Using compensation helps children develop their number sense, rather than merely follow the steps of an algorithm that they may or may not completely understand. Compensation can be applied to any mathematical operation involving whole numbers, fractions, or decimals.

57) FACT IN MY POCKET

"Fact in My Pocket" is a novel, effective strategy that children can use when they are trying to commit some piece of academic content to memory. I have employed this strategy primarily to help students learn their math facts, but I also recommend this approach when kids are trying to learn spelling words, vocabulary words, and science terms.

To incorporate this strategy, students will need two index cards or strips of paper, along with two pockets. Assume, for example, that Jordy needs to learn her multiplication facts. She begins by identifying the two facts that she finds most difficult and then writes the facts on the strips, one fact per strip. As she heads to school in the morning, she puts one strip in her left pocket and the other in her right.

Throughout the day, she takes out the strips to practice the facts. If she does this before school, at recess, at lunch, and after school, she will most likely know these two facts by the end of the day. The next day she can repeat the process with two other difficult facts. Were she to use this strategy every day for a week, she would master ten facts. Students and parents appreciate the novelty and ease of this approach, and the results are worth the effort.

58) STUDENT CHECKERS

Effective classroom management is a necessary precondition for quality learning to occur. This is especially true when my students are working on their problem solving menus because in a typical math period, everyone will focus on one primary activity and then immediately proceed to their menus after they get their work checked. About halfway through a typical period, the potential exists for mass chaos to ensue due to the fact that some students have moved onto their menus and need help or need to be checked with these problems, others need their primary activity checked, and still others need help with the first activity. Even though I am strongly committed to providing instant feedback to each of my students, there is simply no way I can do all this checking and helping by myself. Even with a parent volunteer in the room, it is still very difficult.

To keep everything functioning smoothly, I use a system inspired by well-known educator Sandra Kaplan, an expert in differentiated instruction and author of *The Parallel Curriculum in the Classroom, Book 2* and other books and articles. The basic idea of this system is that students assume a majority of the responsibility for checking one another's work, and that frees up the adults in the room to help the kids who require assistance.

Here's how it works. The first student to finish the main activity gets checked by me. If there are mistakes, the student makes all the necessary corrections. Once everything is correct, I initial that child's paper, and that student becomes the first authorized checker. Assume the child is Karen. Our class has a set of stacking cups, and I give Karen a cup to place on her desk. (If you don't have these cups, any bright, visible object will suffice.) Assume Dante finishes next. He looks around the room, sees that Karen has a cup, and goes to her to get checked.

The cups indicate that a student is open for business, just as the lights in a supermarket check-out stand indicate that a particular aisle is open for business. If Dante has any errors in his work, Karen will point them out, and Dante will go back to his seat to correct them. If his paper is correct, Karen initials the work and Dante shows it to me. I only need to inspect it briefly since Karen already checked it carefully. Once I sign off on Dante's work, he then takes a cup to his seat. The pattern continues until all twelve cups have been distributed. It is important to have several cups in use so that no lines form as more and more students need to be checked. All the kids who have cups are working on their menus, and they pause from their work only when a student visits them to be checked, a task that usually takes just a minute or two.

While the kids are checking one another, I am available to help the students who require assistance with the day's main lesson focus.

It normally takes only a few days for the kids to gain comfort with this system. In addition to freeing me up to provide help, this system affords my students valuable opportunities to develop the Habits of Character that form the foundation of our classroom. Specifically, kids learn to treat one another with greater respect, value one another's opinion, show kindness toward classmates who may have made mistakes with their work, take responsibility for finding an open checker, seek assistance when they need it, and develop the self-discipline needed to make sure they are in the right place and doing the right thing without anybody reminding them.

NOTE

1 https://www.teacherspayteachers.com/Product/Math-Problem-Solving-Menus-398626

Learn Math Concepts through Stories

59) THE STORY OF PERI METER

Movie producer Peter Guber, in a March 15, 2011 *Psychology Today* article entitled "The Inside Story," writes that stories offer

> far more than entertainment. They are the most effective form of human communication, more powerful than any other way of packaging information. And telling purposeful stories is certainly the most efficient means of <u>persuasion</u> in everyday life, the most effective way of translating ideas into action, whether you're greenlighting a $90 million film project, motivating employees to meet an important deadline, or getting your kids through a crisis.

In the classroom, teachers can use the engaging power of stories to help students learn a wide variety of academic content.

When you are teaching content that may be a bit abstract or that kids may find confusing, ask yourself,

> Is there a way I can teach this concept using storytelling? Can I create interesting characters or outlandish storylines that will hook kids, that feature the content children are expected to learn, and that bring that content to life in a way that will entertain the class and help everyone remember the information for a long time to come?

Using this story and the two that follow to introduce the concepts of perimeter, area, and odd and even (and combining them with specific physical movements and/or visuals) will likely do more to help your students understand this content than several days' worth of paper-and-pencil activities would do alone. Here is the story of Peri Meter.

> Once there was a boy named Peri. He was a bit unusual because he didn't seem to have any interests or hobbies. The only thing he liked to do was walk around the outside edge of every place he visited. At recess, he would walk along the border of the playground. At home, he would walk around the outside edge of his room.

His mom noticed her son's habit and shared her concern with Mr. Meter, Peri's father. She said, 'Honey, I'm worried about Peri. He doesn't seem to have any interests, and he doesn't like to do what other kids like to do.' He told her not to worry about it, but Peri's behavior continued. Finally, Mrs. Meter convinced her husband that Peri needed to be checked out by a doctor.

So, after school the next day, they went to the doctor. As the family waited, Mr. Meter read a magazine, Mrs. Meter worried about her son, and Peri just walked around the edge of the waiting room. In the examination room, once Peri stopped walking around it, the doctor determined that Peri was just fine and that the parents should simply leave him alone and take him to have a nice meal. The Meters did what the doctor instructed and brought him to his favorite restaurant, the Souplantation, where Peri avoided the food and did a series of laps around the salad bar.

Peri enjoyed doing these laps, so the next day at school, he began walking laps around the track. His walking turned into running, and the coach noticed Peri's talent. Over time, Peri became a successful track runner and lived happily ever after.

After you tell the story, ask for volunteers who'd like to pretend to be Peri Meter. You'll probably have kids falling all over themselves to have a shot at this opportunity. Choose a volunteer and ask that student to go outside and re-enter as Peri Meter. When the volunteer comes in, point to a table and say, "Hello, Peri, check out our new table." Pretend Peri will (hopefully) start to walk around the table in true Peri Meter style. As time allows, choose other volunteers to play the part of Peri Meter so that as many students as possible can experience the joy of walking around the table. Everyone laughs throughout these turns, but this image of seeing Peri Meter walk around the outside edge of a table is burning into their memories, making the eventual transition to paper-and-pencil perimeter challenges relatively easy. For a visual example of Peri Meter, see Pinterest.[1]

60) THE STORY OF AREA

Down the street from Peri lives another interesting individual, a young lady named Area (pronounced 'AH • re • uh'). She doesn't walk around places as Peri does; she likes to lie down on flat things and cover them completely. Luckily for her, she has the ability to change the shape of her body so she can cover even the most unusual objects. At home, when her mother showed Area the family's new rug, the girl didn't say anything. She simply got on the floor and lay down on it. At school, when her friends played Place Value Hopscotch (Idea #62) at recess, Area didn't do any hopping. She lay down on the court. In class, when the teacher passed out place value mats so the kids could learn all the place value positions, you guessed it, Area lay on them.

One day, Area's family went shopping for a new bed for Area's little sister, who was ready to move out of her crib and into a new big-girl bed. For Area, the mattress store may as well have been Disneyland. Her eyes lit up at the sight of all the brand-new mattresses. Area went to lie down on every one of them. The store manager noticed Area and went over to her mother.

'Ma'am, is this your daughter?' he asked firmly.

'Yes, sir, it is,' the mom replied, thinking he was upset and would ask them to leave the store. Area's mother was surprised to see that he couldn't stop smiling. 'Ma'am,' he said to her, 'your daughter has real talent. I have never seen anyone who lies down as well as she does. Why, she's a natural! I would like to hire her to inspect all the new mattresses as they arrive at the store to ensure that they are fit to sell to customers.'

Area's mom was delighted, and the manager hired Area as the store's new mattress inspector. She became a great success and lived happily ever after.

Now ask for a volunteer who'd like to pretend to be Area. Ask the student to go outside and re-enter as Area. When the volunteer comes in, point to a nearby table and say, "Hello, Area, check out our new table." Pretend Area will undoubtedly climb up on the table in true Area style and spread their arms and legs out to cover it. Everyone will make a big deal about what a good job Area is doing, and probably for the only time in that student's academic career, they will be praised for lying down on the job.

After a few more students take a turn being Area, you are ready for a magical moment. It is time to bring the concepts of perimeter and area together. Ask one student to be Peri and another to be Area at the same time. With one student lying on the desk and the other walking around it, simultaneously, a powerful image is formed in the students' minds, helping them forever distinguish these two concepts that are commonly confused and make a smooth transition to paper-and-pencil work.

You can find visual examples of Area and Peri Meter on Pinterest.[2]

61) THE DAY STEVEN GOT EVEN

This story works well to begin instruction about odd and even numbers, using what developmental psychologist Howard Gardner calls a "narrative entry point" in his book *Multiple Intelligences: The Theory in Practice.*

Here's the story of how Steven got even.

One day at recess Steven went to the doubles handball court and asked to play. His four friends told him they were sorry, but he couldn't play because he didn't have a partner. In a doubles court, they reminded him, teams of two faced other teams of two. Steven tried again the next day, this time encountering three established pairs when he arrived at the court and asked to play. Once again, the other kids told him they'd be happy to have him play, but he'd need to find another person because now altogether there were seven people. Seven is an odd number, and Steven would need to find an eighth player in order to make it even. (While telling the story, use tally marks to record the number of players present at the court each time Steven arrives. This way, students can easily understand the difference between an even number of tallies, where everyone has a partner, and an odd number of tallies, where Steven is missing a partner. To highlight the contrast, record the odd numbers on the left side of the board, the even on the right.)

Undeterred, Steven tried again the next day. This time, before heading to the court, he noticed a new student walking alone on the playground and invited the boy to be his partner. When the others saw a beaming Steven show up with another player, they gladly invited the pair to play in the next game. And that happy story is the day that Steven (literally) got even.

Kids love this story because they hear the title and initially think it will be one of revenge. Upon finding out that the story has nothing to do with revenge and instead ends happily with Steven being able to play handball with his friends after making an effort to include a new student in the game, the kids have a warm, fuzzy feeling on the inside—and learn the difference between odd and even numbers.

NOTES

1 https://www.pinterest.com/stevereifman/teaching-the-whole-child/
2 https://www.pinterest.com/stevereifman/teaching-the-whole-child/

BIBLIOGRAPHY

Gardner, Howard. (1993). *Multiple Intelligences: The Theory in Practice*. Alexandria, VA: BasicBooks.
Guber, Peter. (2011). "The Inside Story." *Psychology Today* (March 15): 79–84.
Reifman, S. (2013). *Rock It! Transform Classroom Learning with Movement, Songs, and Stories*. Saint Johnsbury, VT: Brigantine Media.

Learn Math Concepts through Movement

62) PLACE VALUE HOPSCOTCH

Many children encounter difficulty with math because they don't have a strong understanding of the place value system. Typically, kids either do not know the names of the various place value positions or they do not understand the meaning of each place. Place Value Hopscotch helps students learn the names of the place value positions and can easily be adapted to incorporate as many places as you are teaching. Place Value Jumping Jacks, Idea #63, focuses on the meaning of each place.

Place Value Hopscotch is simple to play. As students jump into each box, they call out the name written in that box. For example, with the first three boxes, the kids call out "ones," "tens," and "hundreds." The next box is the double jump for the comma, and the children actually say the word "comma" aloud as they land on this spot. The last two boxes are "thousands" and "ten thousands." Jumping through the hopscotch court gives kids an opportunity to use multiple learning modalities as they see, say, hear, and move through the names of the place value positions simultaneously. To maximize learning, students need to repeat this sequence several times, preferably over a period of days.

You can make Place Value Hopscotch courts with sidewalk chalk or paint (but only use paint if you have tenure, a solid reputation, and a strong relationship with your principal). The more courts you make, the more turns students get, the less time they spend waiting, and the easier the activity is to manage. To make courts inside, use painter's tape to create courts on the floor. You can even make "virtual courts" by drawing the design of the Place Value Hopscotch court on the board. Have a few students at a time call out the names of the positions as they make a series of short hops on the floor, following the drawing on the board. This last option requires just a few feet of open space.

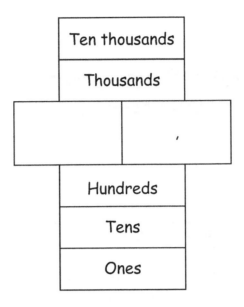

63) PLACE VALUE JUMPING JACKS

This activity reinforces the meaning of each place value positions as well as the place value system as a whole. You will need open space for this exercise, especially to the left of each child. The students begin in the ones place and count from one to ten as they do ten jumping jacks. At "10," the kids wrap their arms around their bodies in a tight bear hug, simulating how ten ones come together to form a ten. Next, in unison the kids hop to the left, showing how the stick of ten must be moved from the ones place into the tens place. The kids then do ten more jumping jacks, this time continuing their counting from where they left off and counting by tens from 10 to 100. At 100, the kids again hug themselves, showing how 10 tens become one hundred. This time the hug is a little wider because they are now representing 100 objects. The kids then hop to the left, showing how the hundred must be moved into the hundreds place. The pattern is repeated for as many positions as you wish. Instead of full jumping jacks, tired kids (and teachers) may do "half jacks" by bringing their arms only to shoulders height. Extremely tired people may opt for "finger jacks."

A chart on the board showing the multiples in each place helps everyone follow along with the activity and learn the place value concept as they physically move through each position.

Place Value Jumping Jacks

Ten Thou.	Thousands	Hundreds	Tens	Ones
10,000	1,000	100	10	1
20,000	2,000	200	20	2
30,000	3,000	300	30	3
40,000	4,000	400	40	4
50,000	5,000	500	50	5
60,000	6,000	600	60	6
70,000	7,000	700	70	7
80,000	8,000	800	80	8
90,000	9,000	900	90	9

64) THE SPRINKLER SYSTEM

This idea was inspired by former Cincinnati Bengals wide receiver Chad Ochocinco, who scored a touchdown one Sunday and celebrated by doing the sprinkler dance. With one hand touching the back of his head and the other extended straight out in front of him, Chad pivoted in different directions pretending to spray the field with water.

I think he must have said to himself, "This would be a great way to teach school-children how to multiply large numbers." I picked up on his message and have used his Sprinkler System ever since to teach the traditional multiplication algorithm.

Draw a multiplication problem on the board. Here is an example:

$$
\begin{array}{r}
427 \\
\times\ 5 \\
\hline
\end{array}
$$

Start by drawing a little sprinkler head coming out of the "ground" right next to the 5. Even better, bring in an impact sprinkler if you have one. Explain that the sprinkler generally shoots water straight up in the air before it pivots, so you start by multiplying 5 by 7 because the 5 is spraying the 7 with water. (During this demonstration you are also carrying numbers and recording them as necessary.) Then the sprinkler pivots to the left and sprays water at the 2. So, the second step is to multiply 5 by 2. Finally, the sprinkler pivots again to the left and shoots water at the 4. So, we multiply 5 by 4. For larger numbers, continue pivoting the sprinkler to the left, one digit at a time, and multiply the bottom number by the additional digits.

Now it's time for you and your students to get up and do Chad's sprinkler dance. Shoot the water straight up and then pivot and shoot as many times as necessary to go along with your number example.

65) THE MULTIPLICATION HULA

This strategy helps children learn how to multiply decimals or money amounts, even when both numbers have decimals in them. Consider the following example:

$$\begin{array}{r} \$6.18 \\ \times \quad 3 \\ \hline 1854 \end{array}$$

Once students know how to do the multiplication (ignoring the decimal point), the Multiplication Hula will help them place the decimal point in the correct spot. Many children tend to bring the decimal point straight down because that's what they learned to do when adding and subtracting decimals.

After doing the multiplication, instruct your students to start at the decimal point and "hula" to the right for each digit to the right of the decimal point. As you say this, make little loops on the board under the numbers. In this case, since there are two digits to the right of the decimal point, the kids should hula two times. Then, physically drop your bodies straight down to show that you are now moving to the product, below the equal sign. Finally, starting on the far right side of the product, the kids hula back to the left the same number of times they hula'd to the right and then place the decimal point. You can emphasize that the hula is a balanced dance and that however many times you hula to the right on top, that's how many times you need to hula back to the left on the bottom.

Reinforce the Multiplication Hula with some theatrics. Wear a Hawaiian shirt and play Hawaiian music in the background when you first describe the Multiplication Hula. After you explain the process, ask the kids to practice the dance a few times. Make it an event—a special moment that kids will tell their friends and family about: "Look at what we were lucky enough to do today in class."

One final note. We hope that students will use number sense to place the decimal point correctly when multiplying with decimals. They should be able to reason that the product couldn't be $1.854 or $185.4 because those answers wouldn't make sense. Number sense would tell you that the answer to the problem in the example would have to be $18.54 because if you have slightly more than six dollars three times, the product would have to be somewhere in the neighborhood of $18. Number sense is the greatest mathematical asset kids possess, and we want to nurture and develop it. The Multiplication Hula is a shortcut, and we must guard against the danger of kids doing the hula without having conceptual understanding. But this tip can be helpful to many children, especially as they progress through school and begin to encounter more complex multiplication-with-decimals questions (e.g., 23.45×1.768). It's a nice trick to have in the bag.

66) THE FARMERS' MARKET

To bring the coordinate grid to life, tell your class that today you are all going on a field trip to the farmers' market. Because you're just now mentioning the trip for the first time, your students will likely be skeptical. (Plus, no trip slips were distributed in advance.) Then explain that it will be a virtual trip right there in your classroom. The skeptical looks should turn to smiles.

You'll need a classroom-sized grid. A large carpet divided into squares is ideal. If you don't have one, you can create a grid with yarn, string, or painter's tape. Outside, you can use sidewalk chalk.

Write numbers on the bottom and on the left side of the grid. Next, place fruit and vegetable cards at every ordered pair. Now the farmers' market is ready. I like to promote healthy eating and exercise as often as I can, and I purposely use fruits and vegetables in this activity for that reason, rather than items such as cookies or candy.

In this activity, students practice the proper "across, then up" sequence of using ordered pairs by retrieving the fruits and vegetables that are placed at various spots on the grid. The first student (let's call her Stella) starts at point (0, 0). Ask her to find the item at point (2, 5). To help her remember the proper "across, then up" order, the rest of the class calls out, "AU, Stella, remember to go across and then up on a coordinate grid." *AU* is a clever variation of the expression "Hey you," in which the "A" stands for "across" and the "U" stands for "up." (With thanks to the old television show, "The Facts of Life.")

Stella walks across two spaces and then up five before stopping at point (2, 5) and announcing the fruit or vegetable on the card located at that spot. If she is correct, collect her card, and she returns to her spot so that the next student can have a turn. If she is incorrect, give her another try. It takes a while for everyone to have a turn, but management is generally pretty easy during this time because the kids are engaged, both during their turns and while calling out our "AU" phrase over and over. By the conclusion of this activity, every child has received plenty of opportunities to see, hear, say, and move through the proper sequence, allowing this concept to sink in and making our eventual transition to paper and pencil activities go smoothly.

Here are two other tips to consider with this activity. First, as the kids are moving, have them repeat both the numbers and the directions to strengthen the learning. For example, if you give Katie point (3, 6), she should call out "3 across" as she moves along the x-axis and "6 up" as she travels up the y-axis.

Another way to reinforce the proper order of the points is by using two simple arm movements. Using the ordered pair (5, 1) as an example, you can simultaneously chant "5 across" as you hold one arm parallel to the ground at chest level and then chant "1 up" as you hold that arm perpendicular to the ground.

BIBLIOGRAPHY

Reifman, S. (2013). *Rock It! Transform Classroom Learning with Movement, Songs, and Stories*. Saint Johnsbury, VT: Brigantine Media.

Learn Academic Content with Chants

67) SUBJECT AND PREDICATE

This section includes a variety of teaching strategies consistent with the Total Physical Response (TPR) approach developed by James Asher, author of *Learning Another Language Through Actions*, that aids students in their understanding of academic concepts through the use of hand and body movements. You can use these ideas to introduce new content, reinforce and practice familiar concepts, and assess student proficiency. If an activity in this section is presented for one purpose (e.g., assessing student proficiency), and you'd like to use it for a different purpose (e.g., introducing new content), simply alter the amount of support you provide and adjust the pace to achieve your desired outcome.

If I use an activity to introduce new material, I will proceed slowly, provide cues, and model the appropriate actions. When I use the same activity for assessment purposes, I quicken the pace and don't provide support because I want to see what my students know.

The rhythms and chants are short and simple. They can be incorporated into your instructional practice easily without much preparation. Repeating the words and corresponding movements helps kids learn important information and transfer it to long-term memory. Employing these ideas for a minute or two per day over a period of days can produce impressive results. After you do the rhythms and chants with your students, you can reinforce these ideas by using them as future Movement Breaks (Idea #90), since the kids will already be familiar with the content.

Use the following chant to help students learn the two parts of a sentence:

"Sub - ject, who or what the sentence is about.	Pre - di - cate,	what happens."
1	2	3	4

Add rhythm to this chant by clapping as you say each syllable of the words *subject* and *predicate* (parts 1 and 3). For parts 2 and 4, turn your palms up and sway from side to side, as if asking a question. Finally, lift your voice on the last word *happens*. Repeat the entire chant two or three times.

68) HEADING OUR PAPER

This "call and response" chant helps my students learn how to head our papers whenever we use wide-ruled lined sheets.

Start by having everyone create a large invisible, vertical sheet of paper by forming the borders with their fingers. Since the students are facing me, I will use the opposite hand that I want them to use to make it easier for them to follow me.

- Point to the top right corner of the virtual paper with both hands and say, "name." Students then repeat the word and the movement. (They will do this after every step.)
- Point with both hands to the area just under the name in the top right corner and say, "date."
- Point with both hands to the center of the paper just above the top line and say, "title."
- Just under the center line, spread your elbows wide and bring the fingertips of each hand together to form a straight line with your arms. Say, "skip a line."
- Take your right hand (students use left) and "slap" the right side (students slap left) of the second line as you say, "indent."
- Shimmy your fingers down the margins of the paper and say, "Leave the margins empty."

69) MAKING AN INFERENCE

One of the most important reading comprehension skills that students learn in elementary school is inferring. When the exact answer to a question can't be found in the text, kids look for a clue that can be combined with their own knowledge to produce an inference.

In this chant the kids repeat the words while performing the movements shown below. Do this "call and response" chant every day for a week as you teach inferring to help kids remember the various parts of the following "equation":

Story Clue + My Own Knowledge = Inference

"Story Clue" – Put palms together and then open hands as if opening a book
" + " – Make addition sign with forearms
"My Own Knowledge" – Student point to their brains
" = " – Make equal sign with forearms
"Inference" – Make capital "I" with their hands: one hand vertical, the other hand going back and forth to make the top and bottom horizontal lines

70) THREE KINDS OF ANGLES

Jean Moize of Action Based Learning inspired this idea that helps kids distinguish among three types of angles: acute, right, and obtuse.

- For right angles: Students spread their thumbs as far away as possible from their index fingers to make a square corner. As the kids display their hands this way, they push their hands out and say, "Right on!"
- For acute angles (less than 90 degrees): Students hold their index fingers and thumbs close together (as if they are looking at some precious, tiny creature) and say, "Ah, cute" (because little things are often cute).
- For obtuse angles (greater than 90 degrees): Students make a fist and extend their pinky fingers and thumbs out to the sides. The thumbs and pinkies form an obtuse angle. The children then shake their hands back and forth and say, "Hang loose, obtuse."

71) HOW TO READ LARGE NUMBERS

Reading large numbers is a difficult task for many children. With this strategy, students incorporate a series of hand movements into the reading process to break this challenge down into a series of smaller, more manageable steps. Using the example of 53,876, the students say "fifty-three," clap on the word "thousand," say "eight", snap on the word "hundred," and say "seventy-six." Prompt the students by writing the number on the board and pointing to the comma when the students say "thousand." Another movement that can be added calls for students to flatten their hands with thumbs touching their chests as they say "two-part" numbers such as "fifty-three" and "seventy-six" to show the hyphen that is needed when all two-part numbers between twenty-one and ninety-nine are written in word form (as opposed to "one-part numbers" such as thirty). To build the habit of reading larger numbers correctly, repeat this process three times for each large number you encounter.

You can use this same approach when working with decimals. Using the example *1.74*, the students say, "one and seventy-four hundredths." On the word "and," students make a decimal point with the tip of their fingers. They make the hyphen with a flat hand when saying "seventy-four." When saying "hundredths," the children make the shape of a very small square with two or three of their fingers on one hand. Because it takes one hundred of these squares to fill one 10 × 10 grid, this finger movement helps students develop conceptual understanding of hundredths. In addition, students can form tenths by extending their index fingers, since ten small squares would connect to form a bar approximately that size.

BIBLIOGRAPHY

Asher, J. (1996). *Learning Another Language through Actions.* Los Gatos, CA: Sky Oaks Productions.

Moize, J. (2000). *Thinking on Your Feet: 100+ Activities That Make Learning a Moving Experience.* Murphy, TX: Action Based Learning.

Reifman, S. (2013). *Rock It! Transform Classroom Learning with Movement, Songs, and Stories.* Saint Johnsbury, VT: Brigantine Media.

Learn Academic Content with Songs

72) "THE BOOK PARTS SONG"

In *Classroom Activators*, author Jerry Evanski writes, "Music can also be used to 'entrain' information into the brain." By *entrain*, Evanski means that teachers can set academic content to music to help students learn and memorize information. The best way to do this is through the use of familiar tunes that authors Schwed and Melichar-Utter, in their book *Brain-Friendly Study Strategies, Grades 2–8: How Teachers Can Help Students Learn*, refer to as "piggyback songs." Using piggyback songs to entrain learning is an example of what presenter Jeff Haebig describes as: "combining solid facts with lively physical acts to construct implicit life-long memory tracts." As with the movement and storytelling-based activities of the previous sections, using songs provides a powerful way for us, as teachers, to take abstract or potentially confusing content that children would otherwise have to memorize by rote and help them learn it more naturally, more easily, and more joyfully. In this section you will find some of my favorite songs that enable kids to learn various types of information.

We begin with "The Book Parts Song," sung to the tune of "The Addams Family."

The title page, table of contents, index, and glossary are four parts of a book that elementary students are frequently expected to learn. In my experience, children often confuse the index with the glossary, and they forget which parts are typically found in the front of books and which are found in the back.

This snappy song should clear up this confusion. As the kids are singing, I like to hold up a sample textbook and display each of these parts while we are proceeding through the song. (I use Post-it Notes to mark the beginning of these sections and open to each part as it comes up in the song. If you wish, your students can do the same with their books.) With this song and others that are relatively short, you may want to repeat the lyrics twice so the kids receive more practice with these ideas.

Some kids enjoy serving as song leaders and stand to form a circle around the rest of the group to create a "surround sound" effect. You will see what a jolt of positive energy performing these songs can provide to your class.

> Turn to the front (snap, snap)
> Turn to the front (snap, snap)
> Turn to the front, turn to the front, turn to the front (snap, snap)

The title page contains / the author and the title
Plus some other info / about how the book was made

The table of contents / shows the chapter names
And the page numbers / on which the chapters start

Turn to the back (snap, snap)
Turn to the back (snap, snap)
Turn to the back, turn to the back, turn to the back (snap, snap)

The glossary is a / little dictionary
with key words from the book / a-n-d what they mean

The ind-ex shows you / key terms from the book
And the page numbers / where they can be found.

73) "THE CAUSE AND EFFECT SONG"

Understanding cause and effect is another important reading comprehension skill children are expected to learn. The two scenarios that lead off the following song should help your students remember that the cause happens before the effect and that the effect cannot happen without the cause. "The Cause and Effect Song" is sung to the tune of "Camptown Races."

My untied shoelace made me trip (cause and effect)
The rainstorm made me go inside (cause and effect)
The cause happens first
The effect happens next
The effect happens beCAUSE of the cause (cause and effect)

74) "NOW YOU'RE AOK"

Learning the names of each part of a mathematical equation doesn't have to be a dull, tedious exercise in rote memorization. Set to the tune of "Surfin' USA" by the Beach Boys, "Now You're AOK" (AKA "The Division Terms Song") will help students learn the following parts of a division equation:

- Dividend: The amount to be separated (To help kids remember the meaning of the dividend, I like to say, "You always start with the stuff you're dividing.")
- Divisor: Either the number of parts in each group (if it is a grouping situation) or the number of groups into which the dividend is separated (if it is a sharing situation).
- Quotient: The answer: Either the number of parts in each group (if it is a sharing situation) or the number of groups into which the dividend is separated (if it is a grouping situation).

The final two lines in the song are designed to build student confidence. It's as if the song tells children, "If you know your division terms, you're AOK. Everything is going to be fine."

> With a division sentence
> You need to know three terms
>
> Start with the **dividend**
> It's what you share with friends
>
> Next door's the **divisor**
> It shows the parts or groups
>
> The **quotient** has the last say
> Now you're AOK.

75) "NEED TO HAVE A CAP"

Nine important capitalization rules are featured in "Need to Have A Cap" (AKA "The When to Use Capitals Song"). Friendly warning: Keeping up the pace with this tune can be a bit tricky. Within each verse, the pace tends to start slowly, speed up through the middle, and slow down again on the last line. Sing this one to the tune of "Old McDonald."

> Some words in a sentence need to have caps (need to have a cap)
> **Days of the week** and **months of the year** (need to have a cap)
> With a Monday here
> An Au-gust there
> Here a day, there a month
> Always caps for days and months
> Some words in a sentence need to have caps (need to have a cap)
>
> The **first word of a sentence** needs to be capped (needs to have a cap)
> With a first word here
> A first word there
> Here a word, there a word
> Always cap the first word
> Some words in a sentence need to have caps (need to have a cap)
>
> **Holidays** and the **word** *I* (need to have a cap)
> Like Labor Day here
> The word *I* there
> Holidays, the word *I*
> Always cap these days and *I*
> Some words in a sentence need to have caps (need to have a cap)

Events in his-to-ry and all **titles** (need to have a cap)
Like the Civil War here
A Superfudge there
History here, a title there
Forget these rules, you best beware
Some words in a sentence need to have caps (need to have a cap)

Special events and **proper nouns** (need to have a cap)
With a Book Fair here
Paris, France there
Special event, proper noun
Learn these rules, you'll wear the crown
Some words in a sentence need to have caps (need to have a cap).

BIBLIOGRAPHY

Evanski, G. (2009). *Classroom Activators: More Than 100 Ways to Energize Learners*. Thousand Oaks, CA: Corwin Press.

Reifman, S. (2013). *Rock It! Transform Classroom Learning with Movement, Songs, and Stories*. Saint Johnsbury, VT: Brigantine Media.

Schwed, A. and Melichar-Utter, J. (2008). *Brain-Friendly Study Strategies, Grades 2–8: How Teachers Can Help Students Learn*. Thousand Oaks, CA: Corwin Press.

PART 3

Build Student Capacity

Improve Student Focus and Behavior

76) END-OF-DAY FLOWCHARTS

Alan Blankstein, author of *Failure is Not an Option*, writes, "Ensuring achievement for *all* learners means having an overarching strategy that encompasses the majority of learners—and then having specific strategies aimed at those who need extra support." This idea and the next describe specific strategies that can help students who may need additional assistance in their quest to meet classroom expectations.

Freddie (not his real name), an organizationally challenged student of mine, had a habit of leaving class each afternoon without some important items: his homework, his backpack, his jacket, and his books. He meant to take all these things home; they just usually didn't find their way into his hands. One morning I sat down with him and suggested that we create a flowchart to help him remember what he needed to do before he left school each day.

Together, we constructed a step-by-step plan, whose steps are shown below. (We taped the flowchart to the top of his desk.) Now Freddie had a clear procedure to follow. The flowchart transformed what had been a confusing array of tasks into a visible sequence of simple steps. (For younger children, consider using pictures on the flowchart instead of words.) The flowchart empowered Freddie to take charge of his behavior. After reading this procedure day after day, he would eventually internalize it, and organization would soon become a habit. This approach builds his capacity while also sparing him some nagging from his parents and teacher.

1) Go to closet and bring backpack and jacket back to desk.
2) Put papers neatly in notebook.
3) Put notebook, books, and jacket in backpack.
4) Put on backpack and check to see if desk and floor are clean.
5) Check off steps 1–4 on my daily checklist.
6) Head out the door with a smile on my face.

Consider using a flowchart any time you and your students need to organize your thinking sequentially. For example, when you are absent, you can leave your lesson plan on the board in the form of a flowchart so the kids know how to proceed from one activity to the next without needing much guidance from the substitute teacher.

77) CHECK SHEETS

Serena was having trouble staying focused at her desk. During independent work time she would frequently look around the room and try to start conversations with other students. I suggested that she keep a check sheet by her side to record the number of times she found herself losing focus each day. I figured that if she became more aware of this tendency, her focus would improve. It didn't. After a week or so, the two of us sat down to talk. The check sheet hadn't been working. We realized that it wasn't serving a useful purpose because it required her to make a check whenever she did something that was viewed as negative. Not surprisingly, she wasn't too enthusiastic about commemorating her losses of focus with check marks.

We then tried a different approach. She would now keep a check sheet by her side to record happier occasions. Every time she lost her focus and then regained it without anyone having to remind her, she would put a check on her paper. Slowly, her focus began to get better. As she saw the number of check marks grow day by day, her attitude improved, and her confidence increased because she knew she was the one controlling her behavior. Serena's improvement also had a positive impact on those around her. Because she was no longer distracting her neighbors as much, they could focus better on their work. She made my job easier as well since I didn't have to keep as close of an eye on her.

Suddenly, other kids began asking me if they could create check sheets of their own. Some, like Serena, wanted to improve their focus, while others wanted to improve a different aspect of their behavior, such as their attentive listening. Because this approach was flexible, the kids could apply it to any habit of character. Before long, half the class proudly displayed check sheets on their desks. I had a check sheet epidemic on my hands. As these events unfolded, I took great pride in the fact that all of it was completely voluntary. The commitment was coming from the students themselves.

78) TEACH PROPER MANNERS

Throughout my career I have embraced a "whole child" approach that values academic excellence, strong character, valuable work habits and social skills, and health and wellness. One of the most important social skills involves using proper manners. The most powerful way for me to help kids develop better manners, as it is with many other skills, is to be a consistent, powerful model. If I want my students to say *please* and *thank you* and use a positive tone of voice, I need to do it myself. Recognizing children who demonstrate great manners is another effective way to promote these behaviors. If, for example, I see a child thanking another student or saying *please* when asking for something, I call attention to that behavior. In addition to using modeling and recognition, we can take our efforts to a higher level by insisting on these behaviors. When handing paper to a student, for example, I may not let go until that child says *thank you*. Similarly, if someone asks to borrow a pair of scissors, I may not answer until I hear the word *please*. Gradually, children will develop better manners as we model, recognize, and insist on this type of behavior.

79) USE STORYTELLING TO IMPROVE STUDENT BEHAVIOR

No matter how well-behaved any of our classes might be, inevitably there will be times during the year when many children seem to be going through a rough stretch all at once. Having a bunch of students experience a bump in the road at the same time should not be taken as a reflection of our management skills. It simply means that our students are human. As teachers, we can't predict or control when these ups and downs will occur, but we can control how we respond to them.

Over the years, I have learned that when many kids are having trouble focusing on their work in class or finding themselves getting into an unusually high number of arguments on the playground, the most effective response is often storytelling.

When telling a story, the key is to feature a student who isn't involved in the incident(s) happening at the time, who experienced something similar in the past, and who overcame that difficulty using an approach that others can emulate. That way, everyone can relate to and benefit from the story's messages, yet nobody feels as if they are being singled out, put on the spot, or made to feel guilty about something they just got caught doing. This approach is non-threatening, and kids can listen to our stories with some emotional detachment.

As the kids listen to me, they will naturally put themselves in the shoes of the featured student, think through the given situation, and absorb the lessons that I am embedding in the story. The storytelling approach is far more effective than lecturing, rewarding, or punishing.

For example, about five years ago a few children were having difficulty taking responsibility for their actions on the playground. When situations occurred, they tended to deny their involvement or shift the blame to others. When I found out what was happening, I immediately thought of one boy in class who wasn't involved in these incidents, but who demonstrated the type of honesty and responsibility that I wanted the other children to develop. We'll call this child Tim, and with his permission, I told the following story to my class as part of our morning circle time.

I started the story by telling everyone that throughout the year, we will all have our ups and downs, and there will be times when we're simply not performing at our best. It could be happening in class, on the playground, or elsewhere. When we're in the middle of one of these rough patches, there are certain things we can do to move through it and come out stronger than we were before. I then said that someone in this class went through one of these difficult times a while back, and he handled everything so well that I wanted to share his story with them. So, I asked his permission to do so, and he gave it to me. That student is Tim. Instantly, the kids are curious, and because the story features someone they know, I have their full attention.

Here's the story. At Tim's parent conference, I told him and his mother that after an outstanding third grade year, he was off to a bit of a rough start this year. His work wasn't quite as good as it was the year before, his writing tended to be very messy, and he wasn't showing the same level of self-discipline in class. After he heard me say these things to his mother, Tim had a few choices. His first option was to deny. He could have said, "No, Mom, this isn't true. My work is fine. I'm doing as well as I did last year, and I'm not really sure what my teacher is talking about." Tim didn't do that.

Second, he could have deflected. He could have said, "Yeah, Mom, it's true. I'm not doing as well as I did in third grade, but it's because my neighbors keep distracting me. Every time I try to do my work, someone keeps talking to me or preventing me from focusing. Plus, a whole bunch of other kids are struggling, too." Tim didn't do that either.

Instead, Tim made a different choice. After I described the situation, he stopped and thought for a moment. Then, he said, "You know what, it's true. I haven't been doing as well as I could have, and I'm going to make a change. I'm going to start working harder, being neater, and showing more self-discipline." The next day, Tim responded like a champion. There was an immediate improvement with his work and behavior that lasted until the end of the school year.

I concluded my story by making a big deal about how impressed I was with Tim's honesty and responsibility and how much respect I gained for him after seeing how admirably he handled himself during the conference. The class listened intently to this entire story, and the ones who were involved in our recent incidents learned some valuable lessons from Tim's experience without being singled out or put on the spot.

As teachers, we can't go back and change any of our students' negative behavior. All we can do is focus on decreasing the likelihood that such behavior will recur. Our goal is to increase our students' future capacity by imparting valuable lessons that will resonate with them. Storytelling is a terrific way to do that.

80) TATTLING VS. REPORTING

In our quest to help children tattle less frequently, an effective starting point is to highlight the difference between tattling and reporting. Once students understand this distinction, the amount of tattling in class is likely to decrease significantly. Tattling tends to be about small things, and the goal is usually to get another student in trouble. Reporting is about serious matters, and we need to encourage kids to report to us whenever they are hurt or if they notice that someone is being bullied or has been injured on the playground or somewhere else on campus. Brainstorming and charting examples of tattling and reporting, role-playing, and reviewing this information over a period of time should go a long way towards taking care of this issue.

81) "FINDING A FLOW" CHART

When many children work independently at their desks, their focus tends to waver, they become easily distracted by other things happening in the room, or they have difficulty sustaining their attention for an entire work period.

Introducing the concept of "flow," popularized by Hungarian psychologist Mihaly Csikszentmihalyi, gives kids encouraging descriptors that can serve as useful reference points. I like to introduce the bullet points shown below a few weeks into the school year. Sometimes I will present this information earlier than that if several kids are experiencing difficulty with their focus at the same time. Periods in which multiple students simultaneously hit a low point are inevitable during the school year, and responding to these occurrences by sharing new ideas is far more effective than becoming angry or punitive.

When I first share these bullet points, I say that I know everyone is working hard to become a great student and I'm excited to show them what researchers have found to be the highest known level of focus, a flow. The kids are eager to test this concept over the next few days, and there's definitely an initial improvement in their performance. Once the kids understand what "flow" means, I can mention it for the rest of the year, with individual children as well as the class as a whole. A cool side benefit of this exercise is that it gives a nod to scientific research and potentially exposes children to new academic fields and interests.

What does it mean to find a FLOW?

- You are working towards a goal.
- The activity is so engaging that other things happening nearby go completely unnoticed.
- You are lost in the experience.
- You understand that something special is happening.
- You remember this feeling and try to recapture it time and time again.

BIBLIOGRAPHY

Blankstein, A. (2004). *Failure Is Not an Option*. Thousand Oaks, CA: Corwin Press.

Csikszentmihaly, M. (1998). *Finding Flow: The Psychology of Engagement with Everyday Life*. Alexandria, VA: BasicBooks, 1993.

Reifman, S. (2008). *8 Essentials for Empowered Teaching & Learning, K–8*. Thousand Oaks, CA: Corwin Press.

Social-Emotional Learning

82) MORNING GREETER

Once I worked at a school that had just built a brand-new classroom. When I walked inside for the first time, the lights automatically turned on, and I was completely caught off guard. I know this may sound silly, but it was a great way to start my day. It made me feel acknowledged, important, and a little special. A short time after that, I realized that if a person was standing outside the door welcoming each student as they arrived, it could produce even more benefits. The job of Morning Greeter was then born and soon became part of our weekly Student Leader's responsibilities. Having a Morning Greeter, whether it's you or a student, not only helps children feel noticed and welcomed, but also develops important social skills (e.g., making eye contact, sharing kind words) and builds positive energy. The greeter can also provide this service after recess, lunch, and other times when your students are returning to class.

Different schools of thought exist regarding the use of hand contact. I've heard of teachers standing outside the classroom each morning using high fives and fist bumps with students, some even creating personalized routines that are unique to each child. The potential spreading of germs, however, is also something to keep in mind.

83) MORNING CHECK-IN

Once my students enter the room and store their belongings, we begin our daily routine with a variation of a team-building activity from Jeanne Gibbs' wonderful book *Tribes*. I was fortunate to discover the *Tribes* program prior to my first year of teaching, and I have started every school day of my 26-year career with the following exercise.

Using a 1–10 scale, each student "checks in" with the group by sharing a number expressing how they are doing that day. A "10" means life could not be better. I am happy, energetic, and ready to have a great day. On the other hand, a "1" means that a serious issue is occurring. Perhaps I am sick, upset, or troubled by something at home. From their circle spots on our class carpet, the kids pick any number between one and ten, fractions and decimals included, to share with the group. I ask everyone to sit in a circle so that all the kids can make eye contact with one another. Students who do not wish to participate have the right to pass.

Going around the circle takes just a minute or two because the kids are saying only numbers; they aren't revealing the reasons behind their numbers, thus preserving everyone's right to privacy. I am always on the lookout for low numbers so that, as the day unfolds, I can offer these students comfort and cheer to boost their spirits. I encourage the kids to do the same. This activity builds a sense of inclusion and mutual caring. It also strengthens the bonds among team members.

Whenever possible, I try to find time in the afternoon to go around the circle again so we can determine whether there have been any changes from the morning. Every now and then, children who began as a 2 or 3, for example, will report that their numbers increased throughout the day because a classmate noticed them and made an effort to improve their mood. My students and I refer to these people as "battery chargers." Kids love filling this important role, and they appreciate working in a learning environment where others look after their well-being.

84) CHALLENGE BEAR

Class symbols offer an effective way to highlight important ideas that we want to build into the fabric of our learning environment. I created our first symbol many years ago when I was looking to help children develop a positive view of the difficult academic challenges that they would inevitably face at school. Rather than worry about a challenge or try to hide from it, I wanted kids to embrace it. A short time later, the Challenge Bear was born. I borrowed a stuffed animal from a student and placed a beauty pageant-like sash with the word *challenge* around it.

Annually, I tell the class that if anyone is feeling a bit nervous about a challenging academic situation, they are free to approach the bear and give it a squeeze before sitting down to get started on it. The kids love the light-hearted, playful tone that we use when discussing the bear, and it has come to represent our team's commitment to embracing tough challenges with confidence—an important life lesson.

85) FRIDAY CIRCLE

Each school day is so packed with activity that there rarely seems time to stop, talk with our students about everything happening in class, and reinforce important priorities.

This idea and the next provide teachers with two effective ways of communicating with students on a consistent basis. The Friday Circle is a weekly class meeting, conducted during the last hour of the school week, that facilitates this type of communication. During this time the kids and I sit in a circle so we can all see and hear one another easily.

These gatherings are held on Friday afternoons for three reasons. First, concluding the week with a class meeting allows my students and me to review the previous week and look ahead to the next. Second, Friday afternoon is a strategic time for these meetings because the last hour of the day before the weekend is generally when kids have the greatest difficulty focusing on academic work. Third, ending with a team-building activity gives me the opportunity to wrap up the week in a positive fashion and send everyone home happy.

A full Friday Circle agenda consists of nine items. Proceeding through every item usually takes between 30 and 45 minutes. When our schedule doesn't allow us this much time—and usually it does not—we do what we can. Typically, we will have approximately 15 minutes at the end of the day on Fridays, and we can complete three or four items. I try to do Recognitions and Accomplishments every week and rotate through the other items over time. Each agenda item is listed below, along with a brief description.

- Recognitions: Students are invited to acknowledge the noteworthy efforts of their classmates. These comments help the kids feel appreciated and valued, positively affecting their intrinsic motivation and sense of connection to the group. Recognitions can be shared either orally or in the form of Way to Go Notes (Idea #30).
- Accomplishments: A time for the kids to share what they accomplished during the week, either academically, with the Habits of Mind or Character, or even something outside of school. Celebrating their achievements helps children build confidence and makes them feel more successful.
- Contributions: Students describe what they did during the week to make the class a better place, such as donate supplies or help clean the room. Such a discussion reinforces the importance of service.
- Next week: In this part of the meeting, the kids express what they hope to accomplish and/or contribute during the week ahead. Looking to the immediate future in this manner whets their appetite for what's to come and strengthens their commitment and ability to plan ahead.
- Learning Connections: Students discuss something they learned during the week and explain how it relates to their everyday lives or how it may relate to their future lives. For example, Aline may say, "This week I learned about the human body, and that helps me because I want to be a doctor when I grow up." Thinking about these connections reinforces the purposes of classroom learning.
- Numbers: As I described previously (Idea #83), my students and I begin our daily morning routine with a brief team-building activity from Jeanne Gibbs' book *Tribes*. Using a 1–10 scale, each student says a number expressing how he or she is doing that day. In addition, whenever possible, we try to find time at the end of the day to go around the circle again so that we can determine whether there have been any changes from the morning. Building this activity into the Friday Circle agenda ensures that even if there isn't time to compare numbers on any other afternoon during the week, there will be a chance to do so on Fridays.
- Solutions: We openly and honestly discuss any problems we may be having and try to solve them together in a positive way. This part of the meeting enables us to continue the dialogue we began during our beginning-of-the-year training period. We use this time to practice problem solving strategies, share ideas that have proven to be successful, and talk about how to prevent similar problems from occurring in the future. The constructive tone that underlies these conversations helps me reinforce the point that the proper response to problems is not anger and blame, but thoughtful action.

- Suggestions: An opportunity for team members to suggest any ideas that they believe will improve the performance, appearance, or morale of the class. Every individual has valuable ideas and should have the chance to express them to a teacher who's willing to listen. Implement as many suggestions as possible so the kids know you take their proposals seriously. Keep and post a running list of all the suggestions your kids offer so that they take pride in the contributions they are making to the class.
- Sharing (otherwise known as Show and Tell): Another way to build a sense of inclusion, this final segment of the Friday Circle allows students to share objects and possessions from home.

86) TWO-MINUTE CHATS

Two-Minute Chats provide another way for us to communicate with our students on a regular basis. Unlike the Friday Circle, however, which includes the entire class, a Two-Minute Chat is a one-on-one conversation. It's important to schedule these talks during independent work time so that we're able to focus our full attention on the matter at hand. I usually conduct mine during independent reading time. Every team member has the opportunity to initiate a chat. When I have something to discuss with a student, I will call them over to my chair. When the kids wish to discuss something with me, they sign up on the sheet I created for this purpose, with the understanding that I may not be able to meet with them right away.

Conduct a Two-Minute Chat to discuss the following:

- Students' progress toward their goals
- Strategies to help students learn or behave better
- Factors that increase or decrease student enthusiasm for learning
- Student suggestions for improving the class
- Any academic material the kids have difficulty understanding
- Ongoing problems or troubles
- Recurring behavior issues
- Individual pieces of student work
- Assessment results
- Long-term projects
- Recent successes or accomplishments
- Any other "whole child" priorities related to work habits, social skills, or health and wellness

For teachers to recognize the intrinsic worth of each individual, we must find the time to talk with each individual. Two-Minute Chats enable us to do just that. They offer a private setting where students are able to speak freely, without worrying about what their classmates are going to say and think, and where we are able to get to know our kids on a deeper level. These conversations increase our effectiveness because, as educator Ted Sizer puts it, "one cannot teach a student well if one does not know that student well." Trust grows, bonds strengthen, and performance improves as a result of these chats.

87) HOW TO FORM TEAMS AT RECESS AND LUNCH

At recess and lunch children often play games that require two teams. In this situation two children frequently act as captains and take turns selecting players until everyone has been assigned to a team. This method may appear to offer a fast, effective way to form teams, but it can cause lasting self-esteem damage to those chosen last and turn what was supposed to be a fun activity into a traumatic, emotional experience that kids remember for a long time. It may even lead some of them to avoid playing sports in the future.

Other team-forming strategies exist that avoid this type of public selection and the accompanying stress many kids feel as they wait to see if they will be picked last. One option is for the children to line up (in random order) and number off 1, 2, 1, 2, etc. In addition, kids can choose teams based on the month of their birthdays (e.g., Team 1: January to June; Team 2: July to December). Children can also form teams based on the colors of their clothing. If two children do end up serving as captains, they should at least step away from the group, make their player choices privately, and come back to gather their teammates so that nobody has to endure a public selection process. The specific way that children make their teams matters far less than the fact that public selection is being avoided.

BIBLIOGRAPHY

Gibbs, J. (1995). *Tribes: A New Way of Learning and Being Together.* Sausalito, CA: Center Source Systems, LLC.

Reifman, S. (2008). *8 Essentials for Empowered Teaching & Learning, K–8.* Thousand Oaks, CA: Corwin Press.

Sizer, T. (1996). *Horace's Hope.* New York: Houghton Mifflin Company.

Health and Wellness

88) TEACH KIDS HOW TO BE GOOD TO THEIR BRAINS

We can introduce the topic of health and wellness to children by sharing the visual shown below. It features eight specific ways we can help kids understand, on a deeper level, how to take better care of themselves or, as I prefer to say, how to be good to their brains.

Are You Being Good to Your Brain?	
Exercising daily?	Embracing challenges?
Eating well?	Sleeping enough?
Staying hydrated?	Staying positive?
Managing stress?	Good relationships?

Once you provide an overview of these ideas, you can post a chart on a classroom wall, share the tips with parents at Back to School Night and in your newsletters, and refer to these topics throughout the year to promote healthy choices. Of course, the most powerful way we can help kids develop strong habits is to model them ourselves on a consistent basis.

Students will probably already be familiar with a few of the items on the visual, such as exercising daily, eating well, and drinking enough water. It's important to emphasize these ideas, as well as the ones that typically don't receive the same attention, such as managing stress, having a great attitude about challenges, getting enough sleep, and maintaining positive relationships with family and friends. For the many kids who face significant daily stress, live sedentary lifestyles, tend to make poor food choices, or experience difficulty in other areas found on the visual, this might represent some of the most valuable content they learn in school.

89) STRESS MANAGEMENT

One item on the afore mentioned visual deals with the topic of stress management. We can empower kids by acknowledging the presence of stress in our lives and determining effective strategies to address it. Every year, I lead my students in an activity in which we brainstorm a class list of relaxation strategies (e.g., deep breathing, spending time with a pet, going for a walk, listening to music) and then each choose our favorite three. We write these ideas on an index card, draw ourselves doing each one, and keep that card on our desks for easy reference throughout the year.

90) MOVEMENT BREAKS

Given the current pressure to address long lists of academic standards in our classrooms, it is tempting to try to pack as much content as possible into every hour of every day. Time is arguably our most valuable commodity, and it makes sense that we would want to use it efficiently and effectively. But the human brain can handle only so much new learning at once. After working hard on a math activity, for example, children need time to process that new learning before moving on to something else. They need time to catch their breath, recharge their batteries, and allow new learning to "settle." Even though the kids may not be aware of it, their brains may still be sorting through the ideas they learned in the last activity as the class launches into a brand new one.

This is where movement breaks enter the classroom. Instead of rushing from one learning activity to the next, take a short break (usually one to two minutes) to give students the processing time they need and enable them to downshift. In addition, movement breaks, because they often involve music, reenergize the room, increase the sense of connection students feel with their classmates, and make everyone happier and more cheerful. Movement breaks require almost no planning, and a repertoire of just four or five ideas will go a long way. We can also employ movement breaks as a "halftime" during lengthy independent work periods.

In *The Kinesthetic Classroom*, authors Traci Lengel and Mike Kuczala talk about "brain breaks." They say,

> The objective of a brain break is to give the brain time away from the academic content. As students participate in these activities, they are giving their hippocampus (the part of the brain that is responsible for the conversion of working memory to long-term memory) a much-needed break.

Children will take mental breaks throughout the day, whether teachers realize it or not, and these breaks may come at inopportune times. When you schedule breaks into the day and make them novel and interesting, you have much greater control over when the breaks occur and how long they last. Scheduling movement breaks helps create a brain-friendly classroom environment in which student focus is likely to remain strong throughout the day and in which teachers can prevent problems related to fatigue or "fidgetiness" from taking place.

An unexpected advantage of planning these activities is that they often give us a moment of set-up time for the next activity, since the kids are self-sufficient during most movement breaks. The kids are moving while we are prepping. That's a win-win for everyone. If there is nothing to prepare, then join right in. (Teachers need breaks, too.)

There are three kinds of movement breaks: 1) Individual movements that kids perform alone standing behind their chairs or spread out in open space; 2) Partner activities that students do with a neighbor; and 3) Movements that involve objects. Using objects requires greater management and a bit more time (to pass out and collect everything), but these activities can be especially valuable in schools without credentialed physical education coaches and where classroom teachers are responsible for providing this type of instruction. Small bits of PE instruction can be incorporated into these movement breaks, and they add up throughout the day.

You may find yourself using movement breaks more often than you expected. Some experts say that kids should be up and moving every eight minutes; others suggest every ten or 20. As you get to know your students well, you will develop a good feel for how long they can attend before they need a brief movement break.

Below you will find a few of my favorite individual movement breaks. You can find additional examples, along with descriptions of partner and object-related activities, in my book *Rock It! Transform Classroom Learning with Movement, Songs, and Stories*. Introduce one of these options, or those you find at Go Noodle or other free sites, until you have a repertoire that you and your students enjoy. Over time, you will discover your favorites and perhaps create your own.

MOVING TO THE MUSIC

This is the most basic movement break of them all. Simply put on a song and let the kids move. If your class is a bit lethargic, consider an upbeat song. If they are overly excited, play a mellow one. Use music to help create the type of environment you want. As the song plays, students may select one or more of the movement choices described in Idea #35, or they may just want to follow the beat of the music in their own ways and to the degree that they want or need to move at the time. As long as the students are keeping their hands to themselves and not bothering their neighbors, the choice of how to move belongs to them. They can dance, stretch, jog in place, or do nothing at all. Some songs that really get kids moving are "Private Idaho" by the B-52s, "Magic" by B.o.B, "All Star" by Smashmouth, and "Shiny Happy People" by R.E.M.

DA DOO RUN RUN

This movement break incorporates research about the positive effects on the brain of spinning and body rotation. Authors Lengel and Kuczala recommend spinning movements in their book *The Kinesthetic Classroom*: "Various spinning, balancing, jumping, rolling, turning, and combination activities can help develop and improve the vestibular system and spatial awareness."

Play the 1960s song, "Da Doo Ron Ron." When the music starts, the students spin slowly. When the chorus is sung ("Da Doo Ron Ron Ron, Da Doo Ron Ron"), the kids jog in place. Change the *Rons* to *Runs*. The children alternate between slow spinning and quick jogging throughout the song.

BEACH MOVEMENTS TO THE BEACH BOYS

Play any Beach Boys song and have your students move to it by simulating any activity that people commonly do at the beach, such as swim, play volleyball, build a sand castle, surf, and apply sunscreen. Students can stick to one movement through the whole song or change movements as they wish.

SPORTS CENTER

Certain songs that have strong associations with specific sports work well as background theme music to movement breaks:

- Theme from "Rocky" ("Gonna Fly Now" by Bill Conti): Students pretend to box, do push-ups, run through the streets of Philadelphia, and eat glasses of raw eggs for breakfast.
- "Sweet Georgia Brown" (The Harlem Globetrotters theme): Kids perform various basketball skills, such as shooting, dribbling, passing, and fancy ball handling.
- "Centerfield" by John Fogerty: Baseball season doesn't officially start each spring until this classic shows up on the radio. Kids run, throw, catch, and swing for the fences.
- "Chariots of Fire": Students jog in place to the theme from this classic film.
- "The Olympics Theme": This song applies to all the events included in the Olympic Games and gives kids numerous movement choices to act out.

---

91) SWITCH LOCATIONS IN THE ROOM HALFWAY THROUGH THE PERIOD

This idea works well when students would otherwise be sitting for an extended period of time doing independent reading, writing, or other seat work. About halfway through the period, ask everyone to stand up, gather their materials, and move to a different spot on the other side of the classroom. This transition gives the kids a chance to take a short break, stretch their legs, and reenergize for the remainder of the activity. Encourage everyone to move quickly and use their best judgment as to who their new neighbors will be.

---

92) WALK AND TALK

Walk and Talk can be used either as a movement break or as part of an academic lesson. To employ the strategy as a movement break, have students walk in pairs around a track or around the room to talk about a variety of topics that you pose, such as their favorite subjects, favorite movies, favorite sports, or favorite games. Every time the children start a new lap, present a new topic. For example, as the whole group prepares to begin its first lap, you can call out, "Discuss your favorite movie and why it's your favorite movie." Prior to the second lap, announce, "Discuss your favorite sport and why it's your favorite sport." Later, you can shorten the instructions and simply say, for example, "Favorite color and why."

You can also choose an academic topic that relates to an activity you recently concluded so that the Walk and Talk can be part of the lesson closure and offer an opportunity for reflection to further cement the learning. For example, if you just finished a math activity in which the kids chose strategies to solve open-ended problems, you can have everyone talk about which strategy they felt was most effective and why.

The Walk and Talk can also be used during instructional lessons as an effective variation of the traditional think-pair-share strategy in which students have time to think privately about an idea, turn and talk to a partner about it, and then participate in a whole-class share. During the "pair" part, instead of having the kids turn and talk with a neighbor, you can ask them to walk and talk with a neighbor. Shy or quiet children tend to be more likely to participate in pair conversations when everyone is spread out and moving throughout the room than when they're seated in close proximity to one another. This activity allows kids to get some exercise and be social.

93) MINDFULNESS MINUTES

Mindfulness activities are becoming increasingly popular in elementary classrooms. There are many approaches, resources, and strategies available to teachers these days, and if you're interested in bringing mindfulness to your students, it can be difficult to know where to begin. I suggest starting with a simple daily exercise that my colleagues and I refer to as "mindfulness minutes." Right after lunch is a great time to incorporate mindfulness minutes into your schedule because after being outside and running around, many students have trouble settling back into class and finding their focus, and they appreciate the opportunity to calm themselves.

Turn off the lights and have relaxing music playing as the kids quietly enter the room. I have my students sit tall on the rug in a cross-legged position with their forearms on their thighs, palms facing upward, and eyes closed. You can also allow the kids to sit at their desks, but I prefer to have everyone together on the rug to promote better posture and eliminate the distractions that children often find in their desks.

Aim for one minute the first couple times you use mindfulness minutes and gradually increase from there until you get to five minutes. During this time, encourage the kids to focus on their inhales and exhales. I tell everyone that when our minds start thinking about other things, which they inevitably do, we want to let those thoughts drift away and return the focus to our breath.

Mindfulness time can be uncomfortable for many students, and they may initially resist our efforts. Encourage these students to try other options until they find one that works for them and serves a positive purpose. Some kids enjoy the challenge of trying to lengthen their inhales and exhales, while others choose to visit their "happy places," such as the beach, the park, or anywhere else that puts them in a good mood. (Mine is Maui.)

You will notice a significant, immediate difference in your students' focus when mindfulness time ends and you move to the next academic activity. The first few times I tried mindfulness minutes, I was amazed by how much more relaxed and productive the kids were and how they worked with greater stamina. Since I do the breathing exercise along with the kids, I, too, am calmer and more relaxed. As a result, I am more mindful in my subsequent interactions with the children.

Once you reach a comfort level with this practice, consider using it first thing in the morning, after recess, or any other time you feel your class would benefit from a few moments of deep breathing.

Over time, transfer becomes the goal. I joke with my students that even though the mindful breathing we do after lunch is helpful, we don't want to be mindful for only five minutes per day. Rather, we want to be mindful *throughout* the day. For example, during our Morning Check-In (Idea #83), we don't want to be whispering to our neighbors or drifting off when others are saying their numbers. We want to be mindful of all our classmates when it's their turn so we can see who might be in need of a boost. Look for additional opportunities to integrate this vocabulary into academic activities and class routines.

94) HAPPINESS PROJECT

In 2011, Shawn Achor, CEO of Good Think Inc., delivered an inspiring TED Talk entitled "The Happy Secret to Better Work." A big idea in his 12-minute presentation[1] is that in our society people tend to believe that we should work hard in order to be happy. Achor suggests that this way of thinking could be backwards. He argues that happiness makes us more productive, creative, and successful. In short, happiness should come first. At the end of his talk, Achor shares suggestions that people can use to focus on the positive aspects of their lives and become happier.

My favorite suggestion is one that I've used with my students for the past few years. Achor asserts that individuals who try this idea for 21 straight days can train themselves to think differently about their lives and actually re-wire their brains. I don't think Achor was speaking specifically to a group of educators, but I think teachers everywhere can benefit from his approach.

His idea involves thinking of three things in our lives for which we are grateful. Each day we think of three new ideas, and over time we realize just how much we have in our lives to be grateful for. For three weeks each year, I conduct this "Happiness Project" at the end of our morning movement warmup routine. I give everyone a minute of quiet think time to come up with their "three gratitudes" and then ask for volunteers to share one or more of their ideas with the class.

During the first few days, volunteers tend to mention such things as family, friends, school, food, and shelter. I originally thought the kids might have difficulty generating new ideas after the first week, but this has never happened. Instead, when we encourage everyone to think more deeply and focus on various aspects of their lives, large and small, they share amazing gratitudes.

I have seen the Happiness Project lead to positive changes in students' moods, attitudes, and productivity, especially with kids who have a tendency of pouting and complaining when things don't go their way. Of course, informing parents about this project and encouraging follow-up at home strengthens the power of this activity.

There are three "teaching moves" I make when leading this exercise that I believe yield important benefits. First, when I introduce the activity each morning, I start by announcing the "day number" and the number of ideas we have generated thus far. On Day 10, for example, I say that we are thinking of gratitudes 28, 29, and 30. That seems to resonate with the kids, and I think they realize to a greater degree how fortunate we all are when we can find that many positive things in our lives.

Second, I try to share examples from my own life. One time I told the kids that I was at a concert the night before and felt so happy to see one of my favorite bands. Right at that moment, I thought of three things about that night that made me grateful, and I was excited to share them the next day in class. When the kids heard that I planned my list the night before, they got excited and came in the next couple days with great ideas ready to share.

Finally, during the three weeks of our Happiness Project, any time I meet one-on-one with students who appear to be sad or lacking confidence, I don't start talking about the task at hand right away. Instead, I first ask them to tell me their three gratitudes from that morning. Doing that seems to bolster their spirits, and then we can address the school work.

When the initiative concludes, we can use it as a reference point for the remainder of the year. I am a big believer in establishing reference points in the classroom to give important ideas a sense of performance. Our Happiness Project is now something we can revisit on a regular basis to help us build and maintain a sense of gratitude in our lives. During those inevitable times when things don't go our way and the bad seems to outweigh the good, we can remember coming up with 45 positive things for which each of us feel grateful. The goal is for that experience to help us ride out the challenging times and maintain a positive attitude, even when it can be difficult to do so.

95) HUMAN HEALTH HUNT

A variation of the well-known "People Hunt" activity found in Jeanne Gibbs' book *Tribes*, the Human Health Hunt contains a list of sentences that connect to various healthy habits and behaviors. The object of the activity is for students to walk around the room and collect the signatures of classmates who exemplify one or more of these behaviors. I stipulate that each child can sign a given paper only once, thus ensuring that everyone mingles with as many people as possible. The Human Health Hunt promotes positive social interactions, creates situations where students need to help one another, and raises awareness of important health concepts. I like to end the activity with a whole-class debrief so that everyone has a chance to share the items which they were able to sign. Jeff Haebig uses the Human Health Hunt in his workshops. A sample Human Health Hunt follows. You can find a printable one on Routledge.com.

112 Build Student Capacity

Name _____

Human Health Hunt

1. _____ doesn't add salt to food.
2. _____ exercises daily or almost daily to stay in shape.
3. _____ regularly eats a healthy breakfast.
4. _____ fastens their seat belt whenever they are in a car.
5. _____ is careful not to eat too much sugar.
6. _____ loves being a student.
7. _____ wears sunscreen to protect their skin.
8. _____ will always be a non-smoker.
9. _____ regularly reads for pleasure.
10. _____ likes wheat bread more than white bread.
11. _____ enjoys a good, hard workout.
12. _____ flosses every day.
13. _____ owns or has owned a furry pet.
14. _____ tries to avoid fried and fatty foods.
15. _____ has looked forward to the start of school.
16. _____ is an enthusiastic swimmer.
17. _____ has given up an unhealthy habit.
18. _____ is careful not to drink too many soft drinks.
19. _____ likes at least two vegetables.
20. _____ tries to think positively at all times.

NOTE

1   http://www.ted.com/talks/shawn_achor_the_happy_secret_to_better_work.html

BIBLIOGRAPHY

Gibbs, J. (1995). *Tribes: A New Way of Learning and Being Together*. Sausalito, CA: Center Source Systems, LLC.

Lengel, T. and Kuczala, M. (2010). *The Kinesthetic Classroom: Teaching and Learning Through Movement*. Thousand Oaks, CA: Corwin Press.

Reifman, S. (2013). *Rock It! Transform Classroom Learning with Movement, Songs, and Stories*. Saint Johnsbury, VT: Brigantine Media.

Goal setting, Reflection, and Self-Evaluation

96) DAILY GOALS

At the end of our morning movement warmup, I ask my students to close their eyes and set a goal for the day that's connected to a habit of character, work habit, or social skill. This type of informal goal setting can be incredibly beneficial because it asks the kids to look ahead. Many times, when teachers bring up the issue of behavior, it's because someone just got caught doing something negative. When I mention the habits first thing in the morning, however, nobody feels as if they are being put on the spot as a consequence of poor behavior. Proactive goal setting is about planting a positive seed in our minds. Since all eyes are closed during this time, I can walk around and check in privately with individual students about various behavioral issues they may be having and offer encouragement.

Setting a goal in this manner helps each student identify the area in which successful performance will make the biggest difference in his or her day. For example, if I know that my greatest difficulty in school involves working with others, I will set a goal about cooperation and think about the specific steps I need to take to make that happen. If maintaining eye contact during instructional lessons is something with which I struggle, I will make that my goal. This process is quick, private, personalized, and allows everyone to start the day on a positive note. Plus, it teaches a valuable life lesson—when we experience difficulty in a given area, we need to commit ourselves to addressing that area. We don't try to hide from it or pretend the issue doesn't exist. Adding an element of reflection and goal setting to our mornings is an important step in facilitating student improvement.

97) METACOGNITION MINI-LESSON

Helping children better understand their own thinking processes is an important teaching goal. The formal name of this topic is metacognition, and at first, it may seem a bit advanced for elementary school children. We can simplify matters, however, by giving our students an opportunity to participate in a "Metacognition Mini-Lesson." This engaging, user-friendly exercise introduces the idea of "thinking about our thinking" in a way that makes sense to kids.

I schedule this activity at the beginning of each school year, but there's never a bad time for it. I begin by holding up a paper with a closed, curvy shape drawn on it that I want to cut out. (I have a class set of these sheets prepared in advance.) I then share that there are basically two ways I can complete the task. The first is called "closed door" thinking, in which the door to my mind is shut. As I begin to cut the shape, I have a strategy, but the kids don't know what it is because I'm not saying anything. I'm not sharing my thinking aloud. I'm just quietly cutting.

The second way is known as "open door" thinking. In this situation I am talking as I cut. I say things such as, "I need to turn the paper right now so I can get a better angle for the scissors. Then, I grab it over here and turn it this way."

After I demonstrate both types of thinking, the kids have an opportunity to work in pairs to try each one out for themselves. First, I instruct everyone to close the door to their minds and cut quietly. Then, I ask one partner at a time to open the door to their thinking and explain their system for cutting the shape from the paper. In all, the introduction, demonstration, and partner practice take no more than five to ten minutes.

The cutting activity is incredibly valuable because it provides us with vocabulary we can use for the rest of the year as we apply the terms to math problem solving and other academic work in which the kids use different strategies to complete a task. I let everyone know that there will be many times throughout the year when we open the door to our thinking and either talk about or write about our strategies to help us understand which ones worked well, which ones didn't, and what lessons we can learn and apply to the future. The "open door" concept helps children reflect on their thinking processes, analyze the strategies they use in class, and get to know themselves as learners on a deeper level.

98) MATH SELF-ASSESSMENTS

When an Olympic athlete such as Michael Phelps earns a gold medal, his moment of triumph doesn't necessarily occur the second he finishes a given race, looks up at the scoreboard, and sees his name at the top. Rather, his victory was earned during those hours of training when he pushed himself to maximize his potential, those times when he built on his strengths and addressed the areas that weren't yet his strengths. It was the sum total of his private preparation that led to his public victory.

The same principle holds true for students. For example, to earn a high score on a math assessment, they need to do well the day of the assessment, of course, but more important than that is what they do in the days and weeks leading up to it. Focusing well during each lesson, working hard on their problem sets and homework, asking for help when they need it, and spending extra time practicing the skills that don't come as easily for them are the private, "building block" moments that make getting a high score possible.

To help students understand these points, I have them complete a quick, daily selfevaluation at the end of each math period. On their unit cover sheet, the kids write the date and lesson number and circle the score that best describes their understanding of the day's skills and concepts. Each point in our four-point scale (below) has a specific meaning. In the "Location" space, the kids indicate whether they are putting their problem set in their math folder or their spot in our Classroom Display Case (Idea #28). At the bottom, there's a place to record any notes they want to remember when it comes to study for our unit assessment. You can find a sample cover sheet below. A printable version is available at Routledge.com.

Determining and analyzing their scores helps students monitor their learning and know when to seek additional assistance or put in a little extra time on that night's homework.

How Did It Go?			
1	2	3	4
This is new to me. I don't get it at all.	I get it a little bit. I'm close to understanding.	I understand it well.	I can teach others.

Name _____

Place Value Unit Cover Sheet

Date	Topic	Self-Evaluation	Location
_____	_____	1 2 3 4	_____
_____	_____	1 2 3 4	_____
_____	_____	1 2 3 4	_____
_____	_____	1 2 3 4	_____
_____	_____	1 2 3 4	_____
_____	_____	1 2 3 4	_____
_____	_____	1 2 3 4	_____
_____	_____	1 2 3 4	_____
_____	_____	1 2 3 4	_____
_____	_____	1 2 3 4	_____

Comments, Notes, Reminders: _____

_____

_____

99) REFLECTION SHEETS

After my students complete a Writing Workshop project, I ask them to reflect on their work and begin thinking ahead to their next project. Reflecting on their writing improves their metacognitive skills, heightens awareness of their strengths, and helps them identify areas of improvement. Because of time constraints, this type of reflection often gets put on the back burner, so it's important to build these activities into your unit plans from the start. The reflection paper typically has four to five questions and follows a certain structure. One question always has a "feel good" quality to it, such as "What is your favorite part of this project?" or "What part of your project makes you the proudest?" Another asks about the greatest challenge or difficulty the kids encountered as they worked through the writing process. "What did you learn about yourself as a writer during this project?" is a great question to include because it requires students to think deeply and encourages them to monitor their learning. An additional question is: "What are your next steps as a writer?" This question helps children look ahead to their next project and determine a specific way they can make that project a little better than their last. This sheet serves as an example of how metacognitive activities enable us to keep one eye on the present and the other on the future so that we can build students' capacity. I include a sample reflection sheet on the following page and on Routledge.com. (You can find a full set of Writing Workshop reflection sheets on my TeachersPayTeachers page.)

Name _____ Date _____

Personal Narrative Reflection Sheet

<u>Directions</u>: Answer the following questions as honestly and thoughtfully as you can. Be sure to write in complete sentences.

1) What are the greatest strengths of your story?

_____

_____

_____

2) What did you learn about yourself as a writer from working on this story?

_____

_____

_____

3) What was the most challenging part of writing this story?

_____

_____

4) What are the most valuable writing skills you learned during this project?

_____

_____

5) What are your next steps as a writer? In other words, what parts of your writing are you the most determined to improve in your next project?

_____

_____

100) PLUS/DELTA CHARTS

I once heard someone remark, "Man knows everything about his work, except how to improve it. After all, if he knew how to improve it, he would be doing it already." This is where feedback helps us. When we are sincerely trying to improve in a given area but are unsure how to do so, we benefit from the expertise, experience, and wisdom of others. As author Stephen Covey puts it in his book *First Things First*, "getting other perspectives will help us improve the quality of our own."

In an empowering classroom environment, feedback takes many forms and flows in many directions. Most commonly, feedback flows from teacher to student. This type of feedback allows us to provide helpful information to kids about both their academic work and behavior. We offer our comments in writing and, when we have time, during one-on-one conversations. Feedback can also flow from student to student. As teachers, we facilitate this exchange of feedback among team members by encouraging them to work cooperatively as frequently as possible, such as during Writing Workshop when it comes time to revise an initial story draft. Promoting student-to-student feedback sends the message that we consider all our kids to be resources, capable of contributing to the betterment of the classroom community. Throughout the year I tell my students that sometimes the most valuable knowledge and skills they learn will not come from me or from a book. It will come from one of their classmates.

Finally, feedback flows from student to teacher. I strongly believe that if I expect the kids to listen to my feedback, then I should listen to theirs. I see this partially as an issue of fairness, but more than that, I actively solicit feedback because I know that the class as a whole benefits from the ideas the students offer. The insights they provide are usually quite keen. In addition, kids appreciate teachers who are willing to listen to them. Feedback, then, benefits students not only when they receive it, but also when they have a chance to provide it. Such opportunities improve their morale, give them greater ownership of the classroom, and generally result in a more productive environment.

Many years ago, for example, the children and I conducted our first set of Student-led Conferences, a variation of the traditional parent-teacher meetings held annually. At the time, I was planning a second set a few months from then in May or June. Though the conferences went very well and the attendance rate was high, I wanted to make the second round better than the first. I had some ideas of how we could improve these meetings, but I wanted feedback from the kids.

I used a simple tool called a "Plus/Delta Chart" shown below to collect student feedback. On the "Plus" (left) side I wrote down everything that the kids liked about how we first conducted the conferences and that they wanted to hold constant for next time. On the "Delta" (right) side I recorded all the ways they thought we could improve our format for the second set. (Delta is the Greek letter used in science to mean "change in.") A Plus/Delta Chart, then, tells us what to preserve and what to modify. I found myself agreeing with the group's recommendations and made a commitment to act on them the next time we conducted Student-led Conferences.

+	**Δ**
1. Liked that they had the opportunity to lead the conference without help from the teacher	1. Should conduct these meetings on more than one day in case any parents are unable to attend
2. Thought the outline was helpful in getting organized for the conference	2. Should include Reading Notebooks as part of the work students show to parents
3. Appreciated the freedom to choose the order in which they presented all the work to their parents	3. Should use technology even more during the conferences
4. Believed we did a good job of decorating the room for the conferences, including displaying all the science projects throughout the class so that parents could observe them	4. Should invite other school personnel, with whom the students work, to meet with parents
5. Enjoyed using the computer to show their parents some of the work they had done recently	5. Teachers should participate in these conferences with their own families
6. Felt that the work they showed thoroughly addressed all the major subject areas	

101) QUALITY WORK RUBRIC

All children want to be successful in school. To achieve at high levels on a consistent basis, kids need to display a variety of traits and dispositions and make decisions about their learning that propel them forward and further their long-term interests. We can offer assistance and inspiration by sharing what I like to call "high-leverage success tips." This information focuses on the daily, nuts-and-bolts actions, behaviors, and strategies that can take kids where they want to go. Many students are fortunate enough to learn these tips at home through discussions with their families, but many are not. Incorporating these ideas into our teaching can help level the playing field and set up all children to be successful.

My first effort to inspire students by providing a "success tip" occurred when I was trying to help everyone dedicate themselves to the goal of producing quality work. At this time, I was familiar with math, writing, and reading comprehension rubrics, but I had never seen one that transcended subject-area boundaries and that, because of its flexibility, could serve as an effective reference point for my classroom throughout the year. Rather than highlight the criteria needed to earn a top score on a specific project or assessment, I wanted a rubric that helped children understand the relationship between the work itself and the attitudes and ingredients needed to produce quality.

Below you will find the rubric I created and continue to use to this day. (I include a printable copy on Routledge.com.) By presenting the rubric to our students, discussing its criteria, posting it, referring to it before the start of new projects, and sharing it with parents, we greatly increase the kids' commitment and their ability to achieve quality in the classroom.

How do I give myself the best chance to produce quality work?

1) **Care deeply** – "Quality = Caring." This simply means that in order to accomplish great things in any endeavor, individuals must care a great deal about the work they do.

2) **Very best effort** – Quality students give their very best effort, day in and day out.

3) **Take pride in it** – When students produce quality work, you can see the pride in their faces and in the way they act.

4) **Improvement** – The idea of continuous improvement means that each piece of work represents, in some way, an improvement over the last one.

5) **Intrinsic motivation** – For work to be considered quality, the effort, desire, and focus must come from within. Quality students do not need to be reminded to get started or stay on task.

6) **Purpose** – Quality work is important work; it serves a purpose. Students should understand how completing a given activity will benefit them, now and in the future.

102) GENERAL SCORING RUBRIC

Using a common scoring system for class assessments creates consistency and provides an effective way for kids to self-evaluate their performance in a variety of areas. Below you will find the general rubric that I use in my classroom. I introduce it to the kids during the first week of school, but it's never too late to incorporate it into your teaching. No matter what piece of work we are assessing, a score of 3 always means that the work meets expectations, 4 means that it exceeds expectations, 2 means that it is below expectations, and 1 means that it is well below expectations. The "Meets Expectations" section is always in bold since achieving that level is our first goal. I encourage students who achieve a 3 to shoot for a 4 the next time around. Some rubrics feature a five-point scale, but I strongly prefer a four-point scale because the distinctions among levels are clean and clear.

Once the kids understand the meaning of these levels, we can apply them to any subject area, as well as behavior and other academic tasks, such as reflections. You may find it useful to view the general rubric as a skeleton, into which you can insert the specific requirements or objectives of any project, performance, or assessment. In addition to the "General Scoring Rubric" shown below, I provide our "Habits of Character Rubric" so you can see how I apply these levels to the Habits of Character and Habits of Mind that comprise the foundation of my teaching. Printable copies of these rubrics are on Routledge.com.

You can find the General Scoring Rubric, Habits of Character Rubric, and rubrics for Writing Workshop, Math Problem Solving, and Reflections in an item I created for TeachersPayTeachers called "User-Friendly Rubrics for Every Occasion."

General Scoring Rubric

All of our class rubrics will follow the structure of the rubric shown below. It uses a 4-point scale, in which "3" represents the standard. The goal will always be for everyone in the class to earn a score of at least "3."

4 = Exceeds Expectations
- The work or performance meets class expectations and somehow surpasses them or contains something more.

----

3 = Meets Expectations
- **The work or performance has everything that it is supposed to have.**

----

2 = Below Expectations
- The work or performance falls just short of having everything it is supposed to have.

----

1 = Significantly Below Expectations
- The work or performance falls well short of having everything it is supposed to have.

Habits of Character Rubric

We will use this rubric whenever we self-evaluate our performance in any of the Habits of Character or Habits of Mind. The scores will always be based on the definitions that we have for each habit. For example, if we were doing a self-evaluation for the habit of Fairness, we would base our self-evaluation on the definition of fairness: Share equally, take turns, raise hand before speaking (not calling out). Our goal is for everyone to earn at least a 3 in every habit of character by June. In other words, the goal is to become more automatic with the habits.

<u>4 = Exceeds Expectations</u> "Going Above and Beyond"
- I am a role model in this habit that others can look to for guidance.
- I never need reminders from an adult or a classmate about this habit.
- My performance in this habit is completely automatic.

<u>3 = Meets Expectations</u> "Consistently Solid"
- **I do what the definition says almost all the time.**
- **I usually don't need reminders from an adult or classmate about this habit.**
- **My performance in this habit is usually automatic.**

<u>2 = Below Expectations</u> "Close, but Not Quite There"
- I do what the definition says some of the time, but not most of the time.
- I tend to need frequent reminders from an adult or a classmate about this habit.
- My performance in this habit is not yet automatic.
- My performance in this habit may interfere with my learning or the learning of others.

<u>1 = Significantly Below Expectations</u> "Still Much to Be Done"
- I do very little of what the definition of this habit says.
- I need reminders from an adult all throughout the day about this habit.
- Talking to me about my behavior takes up a large amount of my teacher's time.
- My performance in this habit strongly interferes with my learning or the learning of others.

103) THE MOST ENGAGING REVIEW
STRATEGY EVER DEVISED

Many authors have written about the importance of reviewing academic content with students to improve understanding and retention. In fact, an important principle states that when children learn new material during the school day, their understanding and retention of that material increases significantly if they have the opportunity to review the new learning at least one more time that day before leaving class.

When I came across this finding, I knew instantly that building a period of daily review into our class schedule deserved to be an important priority, but our afternoons are usually so jam-packed that I wasn't sure if I'd be able to find the time for it.

Then I discovered one of those rare ideas that seemed to offer everything. The strategy was quick, engaging, and effective. It is now my favorite way to review material with students, and it is based on the classic TV game show "The $100,000 Pyramid." As a kid, I loved watching the bonus round that occurred two times per show.

Horse racing fans like to say that the Kentucky Derby is the fastest two minutes in sports. That may be true, but the bonus round of the $100,000 Pyramid is the most exciting minute on television.

If you are unfamiliar with this show, I am including a YouTube link below so you can see what all this fuss is about. I show this footage to my class on the first day we use this strategy, and my kids get very excited to try it themselves.[1]

On the TV show, two contestants face each another and work together to complete six boxes in 60 seconds. One contestant faces a board showing the six boxes while the other faces away from it. The contestant facing the board gives clues to help the other contestant figure out the words in each box. The contestants may not spell the words or use any smaller words or word parts found in the boxes.

In my class I adapted the game. Rather than arrange the boxes in a pyramid shape, I simply create vertical lists of six terms that I take from the various subject areas we studied that day. I also like to mix in a habit of character or word from our mission statement.

On the days we use this strategy, I make two different lists and ask my students to form pairs on the rug. Each child has an opportunity to give and receive clues. In other words, during the first round, half the class faces the board and gives clues while the other half faces away from the board and tries to guess the terms. After the first round the kids switch spots.

I give each group roughly 60 seconds to see if they can solve all six parts. We'll quickly debrief the terms at the end of each round. The whole exercise takes less than five minutes, and the kids get an enjoyable review of the major concepts learned that day.

NOTE

1 https://www.youtube.com/watch?v=lPhX_rxNZcM

BIBLIOGRAPHY

Covey, S. (1994). *First Things First.* New York: Fireside.

Reifman, S. (2008). *8 Essentials for Empowered Teaching & Learning, K–8.* Thousand Oaks, CA: Corwin Press.

Reifman, S. (2016). *1/2 Ways to Personalize Learning, 15.* Santa Monica, CA: Author.

Learning How to Learn

104) FLASH CARDS

The human brain has two main memory systems.

1) <u>Implicit Memory</u> – This system naturally remembers what we experience, such as the colors of a beautiful sunset or the lines of a favorite movie. We usually don't need to study to remember the things we experience.
2) <u>Explicit Memory</u> – This system remembers facts, ideas, and words. School-related examples include math facts, spelling words, vocabulary words, and locations on a map. We usually do need to study, practice, and rehearse to remember this type of information.

Explicit memory is the system most often used in school. Sometimes teachers and parents think children automatically know how to use their Explicit Memory System to study and memorize information, but this is a mistake. We all need strategies that we can use to help us remember the information we are expected to learn. Many hard-working, dedicated students experience difficulty in school simply because they haven't learned helpful ways to study and remember information. We can help bring those days to an end by teaching children a variety of study strategies.

We begin with flash cards. Using flash cards is probably the most popular study strategy among students. Even though this strategy is familiar, it's not always employed effectively. When learning addition facts, for example, the first step is to put the expression on the front and the answer on the back. If kids put the entire equation on the front, there is no way for them to test themselves without seeing the answer. Children should be able to see the expression on the front, test themselves, and then find the answer on the back.

Trying to learn too many facts at once is a common problem. Cramming on Thursday night for a Friday morning test is unlikely to lead to long-term, or even short-term, learning. I remember making a huge stack of flash cards in eighth grade for a science test and practicing the night before. I got the definition of every term correct at least once and went to school the next day thinking I was ready. I wasn't. Cramming can be overwhelming and lead to a false sense of security.

For best results, kids should go through their stack of cards a few days before the assessment to see which ones they know well and which ones they don't and make a pile for each kind—an easy pile and a hard pile. Then they should practice a few cards per day from the hard pile until they know all their cards well. By studying a few facts at a time and spreading the learning over the course of several days, the progress occurs more gradually, there's less pressure and stress, and long-term learning is more likely to result.

One more tip. Instead of studying flash cards while seated, scatter them throughout the room. Put them on tables, chairs, and the floor. Take a walk around the room and look at each card. There is something about having each fact in a different spot and about incorporating movement that helps us remember the information.

105) CHUNKING

Imagine you want to memorize a friend's phone number. It's unlikely you would try to remember one digit at a time (e.g., 3 1 0 5 5 5 1 5 6 7). Instead, you would probably chunk the digits into small groups (310-555-1567). Chunking means that when we have many pieces of information to learn, we don't try to remember them individually. Rather, we seek ways to group information so it is easier on the brain. With our phone number, for example, we are more likely to learn three chunks than we are to learn ten digits. The same idea works for spelling words. When attempting to learn how to spell *through*, for example, it is more effective to learn two chunks (*thr – ough*) than seven letters. Returning to our addition facts example from the previous strategy, we can encourage children to group certain facts together based on a common characteristic. For example, kids can form a chunk out of all the expressions whose sum is ten or that have five as one of the addends. Once students are aware of this strategy, they will use it creatively and successfully.

106) ACRONYMS AND ACROSTICS

Two closely related memorization strategies are acronyms and acrostics. An acronym is an abbreviation formed from the initial letters of multiple words and pronounced as a single word. Imagine we need to learn the names of the five Great Lakes: Lake Erie, Lake Ontario, Lake Huron, Lake Michigan, and Lake Superior. To simplify this task, we can create an acronym by taking the first letter of each lake and forming a word that's easy to remember. This strategy is a form of chunking because rather than learn five individual lake names, we are learning one word that helps us remember the lakes.

H – Huron
O – Ontario
M – Michigan
E – Erie
S – Superior

Once we remember the word *homes*, we can proceed letter-by-letter and say the name of each lake.

In an acrostic we begin by taking the first letter of every word that needs to be memorized and then create a useful phrase or sentence. Perhaps the most common acrostic that we use in schools is one designed to help students learn the names of the planets in order from the sun—and yes, for this example, we will include Pluto. Using the first letter of each planet, we can form the following memorable sentence: My Very Educated Mother Just Served Us Nine Pizzas. Once students memorize this sentence, all nine planets are lined up and ready to go. Before long, kids will be saying Mercury, Venus, Earth, Mars, Jupiter, Saturn, Uranus, Neptune, and Pluto.

107) NOVELTY

According to educator Jeff Haebig, emotions drive attention, and attention drives learning. Put differently, if we can help kids create an emotional connection with academic content, they will pay better attention and learn more. Over the years I've discovered that one of the most effective strategies for engaging children on an emotional level is to use novelty. The more clever, humorous, or off-the-wall, the better.

Several ideas in this book feature novelty. Yelling, "AU, remember to go across and then up on a coordinate grid" is an effective math strategy because it's probably very different from anything kids have seen before. The same is true when we ask them to learn math facts by keeping a couple of strips of paper in their pocket each day and sing a silly song to remember to take home their spelling words.

The next time you're looking to add a dash of novelty to your teaching, consider bringing in a different scent, speaking with an accent, or simply doing something you've never done before. When children are studying content independently, encourage them to do the same. These gestures turn typical lessons into engaging experiences that resonate with children on an emotional level and will likely lead to effective, long-term learning.

For Product Safety Concerns and Information please contact our EU
representative GPSR@taylorandfrancis.com Taylor & Francis Verlag GmbH,
Kaufingerstraße 24, 80331 München, Germany

Printed and bound by CPI Group (UK) Ltd, Croydon, CR0 4YY
08/06/2025
01897001-0020